ON THE SAUCE
A CAUTIONARY TALE OF BEING BURNED BY THE PIZZA INDUSTRY

LIZ VAN PAY

Copyright © 2018 Liz Van Pay

All rights reserved.

This book is dedicated to everyone who never believed in me. And my parents, who always did.

This book is also dedicated to the memory of Terry Johnson, who believed in this story more than I did, sometimes.

CONTENTS

PROLOGUE	1
INTRODUCTION	2
MAY 2008	7
JUNE 2008	12
JULY 2008	16
AUGUST 2008	21
SEPTEMBER 2008	25
OCTOBER 2008	31
NOVEMBER 2008	36
DECEMBER 2008	45
JANUARY 2009	57
FEBRUARY 2009	67
MARCH 2009	75
APRIL 2009	87
MAY 2009	92
JUNE 2009	97
JULY 2009	105
AUGUST 2009	114
SEPTEMBER 2009	121
AFTERMATH	125

PROLOGUE

Have you ever had an itch that you couldn't quite scratch? You twist and turn, and you just can't reach it? This book is mine. Nearly ten years ago, I wrote it immediately after working what is still, to this day, the most ridiculous roller-coaster ride of employment I've ever experienced. Names have been changed, but nothing of this story is fiction - I'd like it to be seen as a double-edged cautionary tale - one, for employers, so they don't treat people like this, and two, for employees - you are never stuck in a dead-end, shit job, working for literal crazy people. You deserve (and can find) much better.

The girl in this story is ten years younger than I am now, and so many things have changed for me. I've learned, and grown, so much, but this itch has still been there. For ten years! Every time I've thought about this manuscript, I've thought, 'someday'. Or wanted it to be perfect before it saw the light of day. What good is re-writing the same story for the fifth time if you're just terrified of putting it out and what might happen? Without risk, what is reward?

I hope you enjoy what you're about to read. I certainly didn't enjoy living it, but I enjoyed the catharsis of the following pages.

INTRODUCTION

Merriam-Webster's definition of a 'job' is as follows:

'A specific duty, role, or function'.

We all need jobs. We need them to make money to support ourselves and in many cases they are a necessary evil. Most of us would much rather spend our time sleeping in and doing what we want instead of muttering "Yes, sir!" and spending our time with 'the man' five days a week.

There are all kinds of occupations to be had. Industrial, telemarketing, hell, even retail… although the latter can be embarrassing for anyone over the age of 25. My niche is in administrative office positions. From call centers to administrative assisting, it has always come easy… and allowed for Internet browsing throughout most days whether my employers liked it or not. Answering phones, filling out paperwork, filing, and data entry are the backbone of most of the positions I've held. From the age of eighteen on, it has been an easy way to collect a paycheck. My start came in the form of a catalog call center, where I dealt with phone calls ranging from customers wanting to order their new Jordan basketball shoes to complaints from customers who – most of the time – had no idea what they were complaining about. I was fired after a year and a half over a scheduling technicality. From there, I picked up an administrative assisting position at a physician recruiting firm, with little more than call center experience. I excelled at doing more than just answering the phone and pretending to be nice. It was one of the first times I was ever allowed to be in charge of anything other than myself, and it felt good. After over a year, I was forced to leave by a boss who wanted me to choose between the job and furthering my education. There have been little jobs here and there since then, until May 2008 when I picked up what I thought at the time would be a big jump in the right direction: my first office manager position. I would have command of a small office with one other employee, and I was only 22.

At first glance, I am not the first person you would expect to jump at the chance to sit in an office behind a desk with a dead stare to a computer screen on my face. I am covered in tattoos that I oh-so-strategically hide behind long sleeves and pants throughout the course of each year. This raised questions for individuals who had no clue and thought that I had some form of skin disease, but their faces when seeing me out in public were always priceless. Being young and having a different look have been big parts of my adult life, but aren't all of me and aren't the reason for the following story.

In mid-2008, I planned to move from Green Bay to Milwaukee, Wisconsin. To do that, I needed work. Like many others job hunting, I utilized local newspapers as well as scouring the Internet for anything that matched my skill set. Seeing an open position for an office manager at a local pizza franchise, I felt that I wasn't completely qualified on paper but that I could learn and compensate for the small amount that I didn't know. At my first interview, I waited 45 minutes before even speaking to the franchise's operating partner. This practice was commonplace, as I would later find out.

The office was located on the 14th floor of a high-end apartment building, instead of an office building. A breathtaking view of downtown Milwaukee greeted visitors, and the bright red paint on one wall tied the business itself into the space it occupied. Visitors were welcomed to sit on a leather couch, which scrunched and creaked uncontrollably if there was even an inch of movement. There was not much to look at, as the whole of the office consisted of a kitchen, 'waiting area', hallway, two offices, and a 'conference room', which was considered the master suite in other apartments. It echoed uncomfortably, but if there were any more furniture in the space it would have been bursting at the seams.

The franchise's management was made up of an operating partner, two area supervisors, an accountant and an office manager. The office manager and accountant were the only two individuals that had offices in the space, and there was no indication as to where the operating partner or two supervisors worked.

The operating partner was a man in his mid forties named Randy, originally from Georgia and with the accent to match. He had an air of superiority whenever he entered a room, which went hand-in-hand with the high-end cologne that burned the nostrils of everyone inside. His over-starched button front shirts and painfully pleated khaki pants tied in far too well with the Dolce and Gabbana eyeglasses that fit close to his face, a face which also boasted obsessively groomed facial hair in the form of a goatee and 'soul patch'.

Each of the area supervisors seemed a lot more down to earth, from their relaxed approach to meetings and interviews down to the fact that it looked like neither of their shirts had ever been ironed, much less starched beyond recognition. Tim was a man in his thirties who always had a smile on his face and a joke to tell. Shane was quiet and reserved, and it took quite a bit to get a reaction out of him, much less a full-blown smile or emotional response, which was strange for someone in his late twenties.

Accounting was taken care of by Ralph, an overweight man in his late fifties who looked like he had health problems at first glance. Buttons busting on his shirt and Velcro shoes were the confirmation, and he always spoke literally, very much like an accountant. Being constantly surrounded by numbers does that to you – everything straight to the point, nothing left up to chance.

Helen was the current office manager, and was a stout woman in her late fifties who sounded as if she had smoked three packs a day for years. She didn't like me from the moment she laid eyes on me, and I confirmed this by her body language and how short our conversations were. It always seemed very mechanical, even in my first interview. She wanted to get over talking to me to get to the next applicant, and I didn't think that I had a chance in hell.

The interview process was very standard. My first interview was with Helen and Randy, with Helen taking the time to explain the duties of the open position, as well as comparing it with my resume and other experience. She explained that she was moving to California, which was her reason for leaving the job. Randy caused the interview to begin 45 minutes late, and he seemed generally disinterested and mute to anything but the black and white of being impressed in a first interview. I was questioned on everything from my work history to the volunteering I had done, as well as topics like how long I envisioned myself sticking with the company and the history of the franchise. After leaving the first interview, I felt like I had given a good impression, but that they would find someone with much more experience and less wet behind the ears to take things over. Imagine my surprise when I received a phone call inviting me to a second interview a week later.

The second interview was with all five of the current management employees, and was more like a six-person interrogation than a job interview. Each staff member took turns spouting off questions about my work history and why I thought I would fit in, especially because I had never held an office manager position before. Each of them took copies of my resume and following the interview I was convinced I would never hear from them again, though Randy assured me that they would get back to me with a decision sooner than later.

Back at home, I was getting ready to move to Milwaukee and had driven two hours to each interview. On my final day at a temporary position before moving, I was on pins and needles. I had not heard from any of the interviews I had gone to, and though I was convinced I was out of the running for the office manager position, I still kept my head up and kept a positive attitude. Checking my phone every ten minutes for a call, I went so far as to call the office to see if any decision had been made. I was nervous. At approximately 3:30 PM on the Friday afternoon before my move, I received an e-mail job offer from Randy. He was offering me the office manager position for $12.00 hourly, and I would be able to start on Monday. I accepted.

I would have one week to learn my new duties, and it was not too tall an order. I was now responsible for the human resources, payroll, unemployment claims, worker's compensation insurance claims, and all of the typical administrative tasks that came with any other office position I had ever held. On paper, it seemed like a great deal to learn, but I was confident. I was on the top of the world, and nothing could bring me down.

It felt like everything was coming together. I was taking a big stride by moving and taking a chance at living in a big city with two of my best friends. Now, I had a bright new job that guaranteed I would be self-sufficient. I was elated as I tearfully hugged my co-workers goodbye and set home to finish packing on my last day living in Green Bay, Milwaukee-bound.

If only I knew then what I know now. From shady business practices to mistreating employees and cutting every corner in the book, this pizza franchise was run shadier than a willow tree. What began as nothing more than another office job turned into my lifestyle and a nightmare in less than a year. Whether considered a memoir or a cautionary tale, this compilation of events serves as confirmation of how far individuals will go to stay employed in trying times. Many just say, "I hate my job, it's boring," or "I wish my boss would get off my back." Most don't have to feel that going in to work every day compromises their personal integrity. The following story is completely true. Nothing has been fabricated; spare the names of others involved, protecting what honor they have left.

MAY 2008

The first day of work at a new job is always difficult. You want to make sure that everything is perfect, from your attitude all the way down to the outfit you choose. First impressions are singular, and there is no way to take back a negative one. I woke up earlier than usual, made sure my makeup and hair were impeccable, dressed professionally, and drove to the office. Not knowing where to park, I parked on the street, and was 'greeted' (if you can call it that) by Helen, standing next to her white Grand Am in the parking lot.

"You're supposed to park in the lot, you know." She screeched.

Rolling my window down, I nodded and pulled from my street spot into the parking space next to her car, and intended to walk into the building.

"Where are you going? We need to go pick up payroll." The screeching continued.

In the back of my mind, I was asking myself, 'How was I supposed to know that?' but I said nothing in retaliation as I climbed into the passenger side of Helen's car. We were off to the payroll processing office, and I was wondering how I was going to get through the next five days. Making small talk was as easy as pulling teeth with Helen. Bleeding negativity from the word go, she was always talking about what a bastard her ex-husband was or how much her children hated her between drags of Misty 120's on breaks. To be honest, I was not surprised. It sounds awful, but it was the truth. Within the first ten minutes of working alongside Helen, I understood why her children hated her, and was relieved to watch the time tick by.

My issues with Helen all came down to the age difference. At 22, I did things in a much faster and more concise way than she was used to, and it outwardly frustrated her. She was old school; typed with two fingers, could barely navigate e-mail, the Internet, or proper grammar and punctuation.

When we sat down in front of the computer, she constantly complained that I was typing or clicking too fast, and that it was hard for her to keep up. I slowed down, realizing she was having issues following along. She questioned everything that I did, from opening programs to which menu I chose to print documents.

When it came to tasks unrelated to the computer, she still found a way to disagree. As she showed me the different documents I would need to copy on a regular basis, she tried to tell me exactly how I needed to load the older-than-dirt copier (which sounded a bit like a retarded Transformer as it churned out hundreds of copies). If I loaded even one sheet incorrectly, she blew her top. It wasn't a special copier by any means, but it was Helen's way or the highway.

It was the strangest and most surreal training experience I have ever had.

From the beginning, Helen disliked me. I could tell in the midst of the interview process, and was genuinely surprised when I got the job. She disliked me because I was a fraction of her age and once she saw what I could do, seethed with jealousy. While on an afternoon break during my training week, she noticed that I was wearing black jeans instead of the customary dress pants I had chosen each of the other days. She told me that Randy would notice immediately and would be incredibly unhappy if I didn't go home and change out of the jeans at lunch. I did – because who would want to get on their new boss' bad side within the first week? Our breaks soon became nothing more than another launching pad for Helen to recount the sad story of her life, pausing only to degrade me in any way that she could.

"If Randy ever finds out about your tattoos, be ready to look for a new job. He won't like that at all." She croaked. I knew that it had to come up sometime.

I didn't question her and I didn't fight her. It has become a large part of my adult life, and I am used to keeping it under wraps at work. When she saw them accidentally, she always seemed disgusted and unimpressed. She still could not believe that this 22-year-old tattooed and pierced girl was taking over the job she'd held for the last year.

Throughout the frustrations of my five-day training, I took quite a bit from it. We went over how to do payroll twice from input to pickup, I read the state unemployment handbook from beginning to end at least three times, and had everything else down like the back of my hand. It always came easily, even if she only showed me some things once or twice.

On the afternoon of Helen's last day, Ralph had arranged for himself, Randy, Tim, Shane, Helen and myself to go to a farewell lunch at a small French restaurant located close to the office. It seemed like a bit of an adventure in cuisine, but I was up for it. Sitting across from Shane, I could not help but notice the small wart-like growths on his temples, which were impossible to ignore and which I found myself staring at more than once throughout lunch. The restaurant's menu was different but an adventure, with crepes and other typical French fare.

From the point that we sat down, Randy complained about everything from the menu to the fact that the ice was melting in his Diet Coke too quickly, and sent our waiter back more than three times to get the perfect ice-to-Diet Coke ratio before he was satisfied. As everyone else sat with their chairs facing the table, Randy sat with the back of his chair facing the wall, sitting sideways throughout the entire meal. Throughout his negativity, Ralph reiterated that the restaurant had been rated very highly by local news, and that he had wanted to try it, which was why he had suggested it. Not looking into it first, Randy had agreed and didn't even realize that it was a French restaurant before sitting down inside. The walls were painted to mimic the appearance of a French street, with a ceiling that looked to have small lighting to add to the decor during the evening hours.

Seemingly avoiding talking to me at all costs, I was both terrified and relieved when Randy asked how training had gone, and expressed his nervousness at some aspects.

"I really hope you know what you're doing with the payroll. That's something that can never have errors." He spoke sharply, as if I didn't know what a big deal two hundred employees' livelihood already was.

"She'll do fine." Helen assured him as I smiled appreciatively through bites.

When the meal was over, Randy ordered an assortment of dessert crepes, which he asked to be prepared to go, instead of eating them in the restaurant. We all thought that he would bring them back to the office where we would share them, especially after he opened the Styrofoam clamshell boxes and showed us what he had purchased.

Since the office was located in an apartment building, it wasn't much of a stretch when I learned that Randy lived in the space directly downstairs. A short commute and a private elevator were good amenities to have, not to mention all of the mileage that was saved from not having to drive.

Each of us stood in the office's waiting area stunned as Randy brought all three full-sized desserts directly downstairs to his apartment. Eyebrows raised and Tim playfully elbowed Shane. "He's actually going to eat those all by himself, isn't he?" We all nodded and scratched our heads in unison. The only reason we were all so disappointed was that they had looked absolutely to die for (Randy made sure to tell us how wonderful they were the next time he had us all in the same room).

The final hours of Helen's last day had her taking me through the desk, making sure that I knew where everything was and answering any questions I had. I wrote down notes busily as she rattled off where things were located and what to do in case of any number of emergencies. Once the clock struck six, however, her negative demeanor seemed to lift and she boxed up her belongings, spare a large artificial plant and a boom box which she had to carry, offering me a handful of the office keys as we stood at the elevator and waited.

"My keychain is so light now." She mused as she looked down at the few keys left in her open palm. Car keys and house keys were all that were there. As she stood there with her things, I felt bad as I was only carrying my purse and offered to take the plant and boom box for her. I put them into her trunk and said my goodbyes, thanking her for teaching me everything. She gave me her cell phone number in case I needed anything or had any last-minute questions, and climbed into her car without looking back. I had a feeling any calls would go unanswered.

I stood in the parking lot for a few minutes after she left, thinking about everything that I went through with her that week, from wanting to punch her to thanking her for showing me what she knew, it was a polar opposite situation. I wasn't even convinced that I liked this job, and now there was no going back. I had taken on a new position and though I was within a probationary period, I was still convinced I would be a square piece trying to fit into a triangular hole. Eventually, I got into my car and started my short drive home, still unable to get the past week off my mind. Had I made the right decision? Would I fit in? Would I be able to live up to everything they wanted? And finally… why me?

JUNE 2008

June was all about filling in the blanks that Helen left and teaching myself what filled them. I had made list upon list, writing down almost everything that came out of her mouth for the five days I spent with her. This included each step of payroll input to a painstaking list of everything contained in each office filing cabinet. This was so I would know where things were, and keep my post-employ rapport with Helen as minimal as possible. I only ever had to send her one e-mail, and it asked what to do with worker's compensation paperwork and where to send it for processing. After that, I never spoke to Helen again.

As the weeks progressed, I found myself realizing that I was doing quite a few more errands than I had been warned about. My own limited resources funded these errands, and they became more and more frequent, each a longer distance from the last. Each Monday, my responsibility was to pick up our payroll from the nearby processing office, instead of Randy ponying up fifteen dollars to have it delivered. Beyond this, I was also responsible for bringing Randy's check to the bank and depositing it for him. These two errands would have been enough, but I was also responsible for utilizing our meager petty cash supply to keep Randy elbow deep in Diet Coke. Helen used to say, "You never want to see him without it. He's addicted." – and it was true. If the weekly 24 can case of DC (as it was lovingly called in the office) ran low or ran out completely, Randy was akin to a crack addict whose dealer was out of town.

Payroll was indisputably the largest part of my job. Ensuring that over two hundred employees received their cheeks weekly without mistakes <u>was</u> a big job to undertake. Input was into a web-based software suite, and each of twelve stores sent a payroll report generated from the store computer on a weekly basis. The number of employees varied on a per-store basis, with the delivery area size also contributing. Data entry alone took one day per week from 9 AM to 6 PM with a one-hour lunch break.

In the stores, there were three different types of employees: in stores (who handle phone orders, making pizzas, and cleaning), delivery drivers, and managers. There were three tiers of manager: shift manager (paid hourly), assistant manager (paid a weekly salary from $500-550), and general manager (paid a weekly salary based on performance).

Following input and verification, the final step was completed: the sales-based pay calculations for each store's general manager. The calculations were done utilizing three main criteria and one performance-dependent criterion. The three main criteria were weekly sales, labor cost and food cost. The performance-related criterion was based on each store's comp percentage. The calculations were infuriating, and the manager payroll changed each and every week. This meant that there was no way for the managers to know how much they made from one week to the next. After my calculations were complete, Randy and Shane would verify and make changes. These changes oftentimes involved taking anywhere from $50 to $100 weekly from at least one manager. Most times, they reduced managers' paychecks and never knew what they were reducing them for when questioned.

If the managers' payroll sounds confusing, it's because it is. I was never sure that I was doing it correctly, and never got verification either way. There was always a problem with check amounts that I heard of from the managers (most of whom did their own calculations to be safe), and it was always because of Randy and Shane. Empty promises were made to take care of the unexplainable missing money, but were never carried out unless persistently brought up.

When doing the math, several general managers averaged less than $7 per hour for over seventy hour work weeks. The managers were shorted thousands of dollars each month, which quickly added up. Each week, I would hear reports from managers complaining about their meager wages, and there was truly nothing I could do. Unless receiving confirmation from Randy himself, no changes were ever to be made to the manager payroll. This confirmation was never received, and several managers began adding up exactly how much was being stolen from them per week.

At the end of my first full month of work, Randy mentioned that he was planning to paint some parts of his apartment, because he wanted it to feel a bit more homelike. The few times I had been in Randy's apartment, I noticed several things. He kept the three-bedroom space so clean you would think that he either ran a hotel instead of a pizza franchise, or that some serious obsessive-compulsive disorder was happening. Its three bedrooms and common areas were all about look and empty aesthetic, instead of being lived in whatsoever. Located on the second-to-last floor of the building and with an expansive deck that faced Lake Michigan and downtown Milwaukee, it was plain to see that it was nothing but a status symbol. One room was utilized as a home office, one was empty and considered spare, and the master bedroom was never to be entered. There was a large flat-screen monitor in each room (sometimes two per room), an impressive home theater in the living room space, and no personalization whatsoever. There were no pictures of friends and family, nothing that showed anything about the property's renter. Randy was a control freak, and his apartment screamed it to the world. Everything may have been in its' place, but this apartment did not seem like a home.

When Randy mentioned hiring someone to come in and paint his apartment, I stated that I could do it because I enjoyed painting. On Sunday, June 22nd, Randy asked me to come by the building at approximately 8:30 PM to begin the project of painting one wall in his living room. It was just he and I, and he had taken the time to move the furniture from the wall so that I could get started. I taped off each wall and piece of trim, and did all the work while Randy sat at the base of the ladder spouting off about wanting to purchase a BMW. I was sure to bring up the gas mileage, and he attempted to argue and say that it 'didn't matter what the gas mileage was', and that I was 'too practical in my thinking'. If I were driving a car with a 20 mile per gallon rating, it would matter to me! Beyond moving the furniture prior to my arrival, Randy was absolutely no help whatsoever. At 5'5", it's difficult for me to reach high spots to paint, even on a ladder. He had called Shane over to help, and Shane's way of helping was sitting on a chair next to Randy and watching me, while they conversed with one another and completely ignored my existence. For the record, no injuries were had, though I was sure I was going to topple from the top of that ladder more than once. After the job was completed at around midnight, Randy told me that he would be 'settling up with me' the next day, which meant that he was actually intending to pay me for my time, which was a surprise. A bit of extra money never hurt anybody, and though he alluded to paying me I did not see it happening. As Monday progressed (and with an e-mail confirmation of his intention to pay me for my time), nothing was mentioned. Before I left, I asked Randy when he was intending to settle up. With a huff, he went downstairs to his apartment and returned with a check for sixty dollars.

"There... settled."

With my job still in its' infancy, it was hard to tell whether or not it would be something I could handle for the long term. It was cemented that I worked for an odd duck, and that the company was not exactly typical, but I felt like I could make it work. There were definite questions that I had, especially after spending time with Randy one-on-one outside of work. Why did he always seem like he was hiding something? Why did he say one thing and do the opposite? These were just two things moving through my thoughts. Part of me saw it as still being uncertain where I fit into the puzzle, and part of me knew that something had to be wrong here. Everything was a secret, and there was no level playing field for anyone. I thought that I was an outsider due to my age or the fact that I was still wet behind the ears and still learning, but at the pit of my stomach, I felt that this wasn't right. Through my years working in offices of all sizes, I knew that this wasn't normal. I may have been new to this position in particular, but I knew what was typical and what wasn't. This was by no means typical.

JULY 2008

Early July is typically all about cookouts, beer, and fireworks in Wisconsin. There is solace in knowing that on Fourth of July weekend, there is usually a day off and a long weekend to reflect on making it through another year. Having Independence Day off is never a question to most employers, who appreciate a day off as much as the minions loading paper in their copiers and fax machines and emptying their trash.

Every employer but my current one.

During the last week in June, I questioned Randy as to if we were going to be given the day off on July 4th or not. Since I was still new, I didn't have a grasp on which holidays were held with enough merit to take a day off. We had off on Memorial Day without a hitch or question, and I envisioned something similar for this holiday. Boy, was I wrong.

Initially, Randy stated that we would have off on Independence Day, so I made plans to go home for the weekend and spend time with family. On July 2nd, I sent Randy an e-mail asking if the holiday was still being taken, and he returned it with a vacation policy dating back to 2006, which lists only three paid holidays per calendar year. Those holidays were Thanksgiving, Christmas, and New Year's Day, and listed additional holidays, which could be taken unpaid with thirty days' notice. In the time it took Randy to send one e-mail, my family plans were squashed, and there seemed to be no going back. Instead of lying down and taking his rebuttal, I questioned him. He called Ralph into my office to talk to us about the policy since Ralph was also upset about not being given the day off. Randy stated that he was sticking to the aforementioned document, and that was that. Instead of fighting regarding Memorial Day being excused, I nodded and went back to what I was doing.

With my family as scattered as it is in many ways, big holiday plans are not typically made spare Thanksgiving and Christmas. I was more affected by Randy's decision than I thought, as I looked up to my computer screen and felt tears in my eyes five minutes after the meeting broke. It had been almost two months since I had seen my parents especially, and was a little homesick. After leaving us to go to a meeting in the conference room, Randy came back into my office ten minutes later. Figuring he wanted me to do something for him, I just looked up to him.

"Did you need something?"

"If I give you Friday off, will you stop making that face?"

Considering I didn't even realize I was upset until a few minutes after the meeting had ended, my realization of making a face was slim to none.

"Yes?" I asked with a question in my voice, because I was still in shock at such an emotional response.

He agreed, and stated that we would have off on Independence Day. After going downstairs to his apartment for the day, I wandered into Ralph's office and asked if having off on July 4th meant that the 3rd was technically a casual jeans day.

"Don't push your luck."

As if that would not have been enough, just days after returning from the long weekend, I found out that Shane, one of our current area supervisors, had embezzled $40,000 from the company. The only times that I ever saw Randy and Ralph speak one on one, it was over a private business-related topic. I never thought anything of it figuring I would not be given full disclosure. During a late afternoon phone call with Randy after Ralph had left for the day, he shared something that I never expected.

"You know about the attorney fees for the large sum of money that went missing, correct?"

"Yes."

"It was Shane."

After the goose bumps rose from my scalp to my ankles, he provided more information.

"A few months ago, it was discovered that Shane had been falsifying bank deposits and pocketing the money. He stole $40,000."

I was speechless.

Apparently, the theft happened over the course of several months.

Each store was required to fax in a copy of the previous day's operating report, and copies of the bank deposit slips at the start of business the next morning. Shane had apparently kept a backlog of deposit slips, used them to show that 'deposits were made', and pocketed the money. One rumor was that he had a gambling addiction and used the money for that, but one question stuck out in my mind.

"Why isn't he in jail?"

"We worked out a deal. He pays the money back, and I keep him out of jail."

This conversation jogged a memory from the week before, when I was bringing a weekly deposit to the bank and saw two checks from Shane totaling approximately $2500. I was never told what they were for, but within this ten-minute conversation, things came together.

Randy and Shane had been attending secret meetings with Randy's attorney to work out the deal to keep Shane out of jail. Shane was now legally obligated to stay employed until paying back the total of $40,000, and since there was not yet a payroll deduction, this would likely take a long time.

Once I found that out about Shane, it was hard for me to work with him. I could not stomach more than minimal interaction. But it would only get worse. After the Fourth of July weekend, there was mention in the office of a car accident that Shane had been involved in while going to a local festival called Glendale Days.

Looking into the accident via local news outlets, it was more than a simple fender-bender. On one of the last nights of the festival, there was a news story online that stated that a car had hit two men and one of them had been killed. The men were a father and son, and they had been picking up some items from the road that had fallen from the back of their Jeep while moving. The son was killed, the father just injured.

Shane was driving the car.

In a two-week span, I found out so much that I felt my head was apt to explode at any point in time. How could anyone hit someone with his or her car, much less commit vehicular homicide, and come to work the next day like nothing had happened? Something was up with Shane, and it was something big.

He had never been a big talker. Unless responding to something that somebody said, Shane kept to himself. I could not envision how this man was capable of embezzlement and also responsible for someone's death, and brushed it off his shoulders like no big deal. It was a big deal – personally, I could not see hitting someone with my car and being okay enough to go to work the next day. There was something very, very wrong here, and I ignored the sour feeling in my stomach and continued to work.

One would think that without embezzlement and vehicular homicide that the office had enough going on, and I would tend to agree. I stayed busy and kept myself out of the issues, however. If being in the 'inner circle' of this company meant doing the things Shane did, I would not sleep at night.

With summer came higher outdoor temperatures. I was thankful that given my predicament of having to wear long sleeves and pants year-round that air conditioning was an option. Mid-month, it was in the mid to high 80's in Milwaukee and was quite humid, even near the lake. Working on the fourteenth floor of a building, this increased significantly, especially mornings when the sun beat directly onto my desk.

The temperature controls were located in the office's hallway, and covered by a lockbox that I had the key to. I set the office to a comfortable temperature and figured that it might increase the bill, but I was much happier being comfortable than worrying about an energy bill. Randy, however, had other plans. He typically worked from his home office, which was set in the low 70's and was frosty, even on cooler days. On one particular afternoon, he came upstairs and saw that I had the temperature set at the low-mid 70's, and asked for the key.

"You need to manage the air and make sure our bill doesn't get too high." He said as he unlocked the box and made adjustments, pocketing the key.

"It was set at 73."

"It's not warm enough. The bill will skyrocket."

Instead of fighting, I opted to keep my mouth shut. What little input I had given had caused Randy to take the key from me completely, so I was now required to work fully covered and sweat behind my desk. The afternoon cloud cover was rarely relief from the morning sun. I was not about to ask for a return of the key, however – I am a purveyor of picking your battles, and this was one that didn't deserve the light of day. Ralph stated that this wasn't a new thing, and that Randy had bought a clip fan for Helen's desk so the air wasn't necessary. All the clip fan did was blow my paperwork everywhere – there was no relief to be had. Sweat to death or be irritated, those were my options. I chose the former.

Only days later, I was waist-deep in work with strict deadlines, and received a phone call from Randy. He needed me to drive almost fifteen minutes out of town to deposit money in a parking meter for him. Why? He was waiting in line at the mall's Apple Store for the release of the new iPhone 3G, and could not get out of line to feed his own meter. This was an absolutely ridiculous errand, but I did it. Not only because my employer asked me to, but because in a way, I was beginning to have a bleeding heart complex about Randy. I felt sorry for him. I never asked for a dime in gas money, just did as I was asked and burned my own gas to feed a parking meter. I was thanked and praised, but thanks and praise didn't put gas in my car. If only I thought this was the most asinine errand I could have been asked to do. The next week, I was called and told that Randy needed another errand run only this time he was downstairs in his apartment. He needed me to return several items to a local electronics store, most of which fit into a plastic bag, but one item being an over 30" LCD monitor that I could barely carry, much less fit into the back seat of my Chevrolet Cavalier. Although this time, I was given $20 for gas and frustration, as I had to exchange the monitor for a different one.

Since when was I Randy's personal assistant instead of his office manager? Running an errand once and awhile I understood, but they got more and more frequent, and more and more ridiculous. I would not have been surprised at that point if I was asked to do Randy's personal grocery shopping. Thankfully, I wasn't.

After the month of July, nothing would surprise me anymore.

AUGUST 2008

The first week in August, Randy asked me to bring him to the airport. I figured that it would not be too tall an order and agreed. Later, I found out that his departing flight was at 5 AM. This meant that I would have to pick him up by 4 AM in order to allow him the proper time to get through airport security.

Fuck. I was too nice. I was far, far too nice, and not a good enough morning person to get through this alive.

Of course, when the morning came my brain was on overdrive and I snoozed my alarm more times than I should have. Looking at the clock, it was 4:10 AM.

"Where are you?" I received via text.

"Alarm didn't go off, on my way." I lied.

I arrived at 4:15 AM. Randy got into my car, and off we went.

Halfway to the airport, Randy (who had been on the phone with his airline's customer service the duration of the trip) told me to turn around because his flight had been cancelled. At the next exit, I turned around. Randy, still on the phone with customer service, told me to get back on the freeway, because his flight had only been delayed. Infuriated, but seeing the positive in the situation of not having to deal with him for at least one day, I got back on the freeway and we arrived at the airport at around 5 AM.

"Thanks." Was all he uttered as he pulled his bag from my rear passenger door and slammed the front door as he spun and headed toward the ticketing area.

The next week, it happened again.

His rudeness astounded me. The only other part that astounded me was the fact that between the two trips, I had put nearly eighty miles on my car and wasn't given even five dollars for gas, when it was nearly five dollars per gallon.

Late in the second week of August, Randy came into my office one morning. He looked frazzled. He was dressed in a pair of jeans and a sweatshirt, which was very unlike him. Without a word, he closed the door and sat down in a chair next to my desk, rubbing his eyes constantly.

My first thought was that I had done something to upset him. Maybe I wasn't working out as his office manager as well as he had thought initially. Maybe there was something that I wasn't doing that he needed me to. This was less formal than that, though. There was something on his mind that wasn't related to the business or me and I could read it all over his face.

After sitting down, the words just poured out of him. There seemed to be no reasoning for it. He needed someone to talk to and since I was on his payroll, I did not have a choice. He went on about his former lives in North Carolina and Georgia, which included working for the corporate division of our company, instead of just running a franchise. Prior to that, he stated that he had been a police officer, which he had to stop doing after an accident required leg surgery. That was where he got his start in pizza – and as a side note, the accident was where Randy's prosthetic leg rumor started. One of the managers said that he had one – which was untrue, but the rumor mill in the company was akin to that of a local high school.

From there, the conversation slipped into uncharted territory as he talked about his past life as a womanizer, dating local beauty queens and even having a son with one – a son he never talked to or about. From this, he told me what I'd known all along; that he was gay. He never seemed to be dating anyone, and he didn't seem to have much of a life outside of this franchise. From that, he explained that the reason that he hadn't gotten rid of Shane after the theft was that he was in love with him.

Shane was straight as the day was long.

It felt like the nerve endings in my brain were all exploding at once. Why was he telling me all of this? What was it supposed to prove? Did he feel so alone that he felt I was the only person he could talk to? Couldn't he have friends outside the company? There was no reason for him to tell me any of these things.

As a whole, the impromptu therapy session lasted three hours, finally ending at about 2:30 PM. I was finally allowed to leave for lunch. After spilling his guts to me, Randy offered to bring me to the Apple Store so he could get me an iPhone, since he thought I deserved it. It was a bit of a status symbol to have in the company, as both Shane and Randy used them as their business phones. I didn't think anything of it, figuring that it would flutter out of Randy's mind as fast as he'd gone back downstairs.

I was surprised when Randy came back upstairs at 6:00, ready to go. I drove (as usual), and was allowed to pick out the phone color I wanted, before informing Randy that due to some unfortunate decisions when I was younger, I was unsure if the phone carrier would allow me to open another account. When I attempted to open it in my own name, the security deposit was astronomical and Randy just opted to put my phone onto his plan. Nothing was mentioned about the service itself, but I figured we would work it out later. After leaving the store, he offered to take me to dinner. I figured I wasn't doing anything else, so why not?

Since we were at an open-air mall, he decided on the most expensive restaurant there, a large seafood restaurant. I have never had a taste for fish outside of sushi, but I swallowed my pride and went without showing any signs of dislike. The moment we got there, however, I regretted going. Randy was starting to make sexualized comments about every male waiter in the place.

"I wish we would have gotten that one… he's much cuter than ours. Ours is too fat." He spoke to my blank expression and a shrug.

"So which of the waiters would you choose if you were given the opportunity?" He asked.

While the awkward alarm was going off between my ears, I made sheepish comments in retaliation. By then, I was ready to beg our waiter to bring our food so I would not have to listen to Randy talk and make me feel awkward anymore. Thankfully, he seemed to have some form of ESP or our brains were on the same wavelength and our food arrived. The rest of dinner was relatively tame, with me not saying much and really wanting to get him back home as soon as possible so that I could return to the land of the sane.

The actions of the people surrounding me at work were enough to make my head spin. How was nobody coming in to do anything about this? Not that they would have any way of knowing. Randy had everything business related under his own lock and key. My internal battle had started, however – I was given this information and expected to keep it all a secret. How could I, when it was affecting the other employees of the company? I was working for someone who was obviously too self-involved to care about the welfare of his other employees (spare Shane), so how could I continue protecting him and saying that what he was doing was okay? It obviously wasn't, but there was nothing that I could do. He was set in his ways and I was set in mine. I have always put my heart and soul into my work, and had a big issue doing that with this constant black cloud over my head.

SEPTEMBER 2008

Even after all of the things I found out about in my first three full months on the job, I still acted as if nothing was wrong. Inside, I panicked. Even though I am young and don't have ten years of experience in the world of corporate anonymity, I knew that this was all wrong. I should not have had a boss buying me gifts and sharing that much of his personal life with me, or have had to deal with a rumor mill akin to that of a local high school. I shouldn't have had to stand by and smile while I watched countless people get screwed over on a weekly basis.

Randy and Shane's favorite thing to do was hold meetings. No matter how incidental the purpose was, it seemed that was when Randy was his happiest, secondary only to when he was cleaning. My interview was not a one-off in terms of wait time. Weekly, I would sit in my office with on-time interviewees in our lobby, none waiting less than a half hour for Randy, Shane, or both. It seemed like a game – whoever sat and waited long enough would get the privilege of meeting with either of them. The longest I ever saw someone wait was over two hours… for a job at a pizza restaurant! Interviews are classically a one-on-one 'getting to know you' experience. Not with Randy. He would take a copy of a resume and ask questions, but was always disconnected. He was always so busy with whatever it was he did all day that he could not be bothered to put his iPhone down for fifteen minutes and hold an honest conversation. The iPhone wasn't the worst part. Often, he would have his laptop out in front of him, and would ask halfhearted questions from behind the glow of the computer screen. Notifications of e-mails and other sounds shook the otherwise uncomfortable silence of the typical interview process. I don't believe he did these things out of necessity; I believe he did them to show how important he saw himself in his own mind. Everything from his over starched, over pleated look to his blatant disregard for the time of others were two indications that this guy was either clueless or a complete jerk. Being the operating partner of a pizza franchise was not a life-consuming job; none are, but Randy made it one. He truly lived and breathed what he did for a living. Randy coined the phrase "this isn't a job, it's a lifestyle", and he lived it to the fullest: if you can call it living at all.

Part of that lifestyle was working each and every day. This included weekends and all holidays. To combat Randy's insane vacation policy, Ralph and I had both taken off on Labor Day with the adequate clearance. I was looking forward to a day of grilling out and not worrying about work. The wind was taken out of my sails at 2:30 PM on Labor Day when I was called into the office. They needed me to come in for a few minutes to retrieve the weekly payroll out of my locked filing cabinet. When I arrived, I had not dressed for work and was in jeans and a t-shirt. This was most employees' first glimpse of me outside of the typical work attire, and it garnered a lot of raised eyebrows. "Liz, we had no idea that you had tattoos." several of the store managers said as I walked into the office door. Every Monday, Randy and Shane held a meeting with all of the stores' general managers, and within this meeting the weekly payroll was given out. Since I thought that the meeting would take place on Tuesday, I just tucked the paychecks and reports into my filing cabinet. Upon my arrival, Randy had a laundry list of things for me to do, even though he previously said that I would only be there for a few minutes. I wound up working for almost four hours, under the guidance of a Randy who was visibly upset that I had chosen to wear street clothes instead of my typical work attire. I fielded phone calls, answered questions from the managers, and even did data entry and other normal duties, without uttering a single word of protest. Even though it was a holiday and I had things going on at home, I stayed for as long as they needed me, keeping my upset quiet. This was due to the fact that I was still new, and I didn't know if this was one of Randy's understated tests as to how far I would go for my job – as if putting change in his parking meter two months before had not been enough.

As I continued getting to know everyone, I received praise from many general managers who told me that I was better than Helen, which I was thankful for. I also began to see a side of Ralph that I had not known about before. The closer he saw me getting to Randy, the more upset and defensive he would get when we would work together or even be in the same room. He started 'affectionately' calling me Randy's princess, or 'the darling of the office'. It annoyed me and made me feel like a brown-noser, but I already got the feeling that Randy didn't like Ralph and that Ralph knew it. I was starting to get the same feeling about him, as I walked into his office to ask him a question on one particular occasion and found him writing an e-mail message to Helen about how "annoying and irritating" I am, and how I never shut up and constantly need to have my voice heard. On the day that happened, I did not confront him. I just asked my question and left as soon as possible. On other occasions, I walked in to find Ralph perusing local job posting web sites looking for new employment. I understand that some people do these things and don't care either way – and would tend to say that Ralph was one of those people. He could have had a little bit more tact when it came down to it. Once Ralph figured out that Randy had gotten me an iPhone, he attempted to pry information out of me about what my meeting with him had been about and what we'd talked about – surely to forward the information on to Helen, as if it should have mattered to her anymore. By nature, Ralph was a negative person, but I had never directly done anything to him to make him react to me that way. Randy had also approached me and stated that he was going to post an ad online looking for a new accountant, in case anybody called the office about it. This would have been fine, except Ralph found the post almost as soon as it went up, and I was brought into the middle of a war. I didn't know which of them would be left standing after the dust cleared.

Not to say that Ralph was a bad person, because he wasn't. He was almost sixty and had seen many different jobs throughout his years. He tried to give me the low-down on how the company was actually run shortly after I started, but had not been the person to tell me about the issues with Shane. He was more interested in letting me know exactly how Randy was, instead of letting me be cheery and feel like Randy was just a normal single guy running a business. I used his experience in his almost two years of employment to pad the way I was feeling, and tell myself that there was someone else involved that felt the exact same way. In a strange way, Ralph gave me comfort, even if the two of us were at each other's throats more often than we saw the other in a positive light. The only thing that got to me was his e-mail gossiping with Helen. I had never done or said anything to him directly to make him dislike me, and I certainly didn't do anything to Helen in the five days I'd worked with her. Why was he doing it? What possible good would come out of a sixty year old gossiping about a twenty two year old? What was the reasoning? These were questions that I kept inside, but as things progressed, I should have voiced them much sooner.

Not knowing any better, I told Randy a lot of things that Ralph had said about him, that he had asked me to keep confidential. When I was having a bad experience or I was in a bad mood, Randy pulled these things out of me, and like a fool I thought that they would be kept between he and I. One afternoon, Randy went into Ralph's office for a meeting, and I had run out to do some errands. Coming back in, I was just met by Randy, who told me at the elevator that he had told Ralph everything I'd said to him, and told me to 'have fun and not kill each other'. What in the name of hell…? That was a mistake I would never make again. I did the best I could to resolve it, though, swallowing my pride and entering Ralph's office, tail between my legs and apologizing for making the mistake. It killed Randy to know that he and I weren't screaming at each other, and were dealing with my mistake like adults. This was just the kind of thing that reinforced my ideas about the company and its' elementary rumor mill as a whole.

Since so many of the company's employees were working astronomical hours, there was nothing else to do but spend time with coworkers outside of work, and gossip about others while they were at work. The big rumor when I started, besides Randy being gay, was that Randy had a prosthetic leg – which was untrue. Randy always swore up and down that he hated the rumors and didn't understand why so many people seemed to get off on spreading them. After my experience with the Ralph situation, everything came together much clearer: Randy started more rumors than anyone else did, and he was complaining about something that he was at fault for more often than not. It was a mind fuck for sure. Was I working for an adult, or was I working for a teenager? What could I tell Randy that he would keep to himself? Was he testing me by coming out to me, and then seeing if it would get around in the restaurants (who had their suspicions anyway)? These were questions I asked myself, but never really wanted the answers to. The further I got in, the further away I wanted to be.

Mid-September, Randy called up to the office late in the afternoon and stated that he had just woken up after a long night of drinking with Shane. He stated that Shane had brought him to a college party and down to a few popular local bars, and that they had been out late, although he "didn't make a practice of drinking often". At 4:30 PM, he came upstairs to the office (although he lived downstairs) and lay down on the lobby couch, instructing me to wake him up at 6 PM when I left. He stated that Shane was sleeping downstairs, and that he did not want to disturb him. Here was my boss, obviously hung over from a long night of drinking and who didn't want any rumors to spread about him... passed out on the lobby couch in our office instead of sleeping downstairs, in his own apartment. This made no sense, and brought a funny side to what I was currently dealing with. Was this reality, or was this some sort of backwards, alternate reality that wasn't happening? I could not keep myself from laughing about it all in utter and complete disbelief.

For as funny as the situation continued to be, Randy's 'not a job, a lifestyle' comment echoed in my brain constantly, especially due to the large amount of phone calls and text messages I received both while I was at work and after I had left for the day. The phone calls would never be over anything small, either. One night at September's end, he called me at 11:00 PM, while I was at a friend's housewarming party. He wanted to "hang out". I told him that unfortunately I was spending time with friends and could not (not that I would go hang out with my boss at 11 on a Saturday night anyway). His cover was that he 'wanted to know how long the local grocery store was open', although I didn't understand why he called me. He owned an iPhone, and Googling it would have been much easier. After I told him I didn't know, he launched into a long conversation about things between him and Shane and how confused he was, but all the while apologized and said that he knew that I was out and that I was busy. So why keep me on the phone? Just another thing to prove positive that the only person that existed in Randy's mind was himself, Shane sitting pretty at a close second.

Speaking of the iPhone, around the end of September was when we received the first bill with my phone included. Not thinking anything of it, I put it into Randy's mail pile, and he came into my office soon after, to inform me that I would need to pay my own half of the phone's astronomical service. Shane's phone, on the other hand, Randy paid for. Regretfully, I put a payroll deduction into the system, and began paying for my service as he requested. If I knew that I would be required to pay for the service, I never would have agreed to let him get me the phone. More and more, Randy proved to me that nothing that ever came out of his mouth was the truth, and honesty didn't seem to be in his vocabulary.

OCTOBER 2008

As if the insanity of the past few months hadn't taken its' toll on me emotionally, it all started again on October first. Late in the afternoon, Randy came into my office and told me that we were going 'on an errand', but refused to tell me where to. I reluctantly agreed, though I had a pile of work to get through. He was still my boss and I was still being paid to do whatever he wanted me to (within reason) from 9 AM – 6 PM. This trip led us to the local Macy's store, where he needed an opinion on a jacket he liked. Apparently, he had given his to Shane after a night out previously, and wanted to know if a black leather Calvin Klein jacket would be a good choice. He went so far as to make me stand and watch while he put on several. I stood around and sent text messages to friends about how ridiculous this was, rolling my eyes as soon as I looked away from Randy and was out of his field of vision. At the end of it all, he didn't wind up leaving with a jacket and I could not help but think of how stupid it had been, but being thankful that he hadn't made me drive. At the same time, I wished that I had. Randy drove recklessly from the point we got on the freeway for the trip's duration – speeding, changing lanes erratically and all-around being an asshole to other motorists. The conversation somehow drifted to our African-American employees, who he affectionately referred to by using the 'n' word, which made me instantly uncomfortable and left me gripping to the door handle angrily. I had been raised to treat everyone equally, but uttering that word was enough to set me off. He was my boss and this wasn't possible. I resorted to silence.

Thankful to be back to the office after an unnecessary shopping trip, we got upstairs to a frazzled Shane, who had just called the police on a former employee. He had been in a meeting with the employee and confronted him about theft at his store. The theft had taken place by the employee discounting food on credit card orders and increasing the tip. This allowed him to pocket the tip money, to the tune of around $1,000. Shane attempted to force the employee to sign over the check as beginning payback, which he had refused to do. Not only refusing, he grabbed the check off of the table at his first opportunity and ran out of the office, and Shane was unable to catch him. Shane called the police to file a report, and I was asked to speak to them as if I had been present for the meeting. I refused; as I had seen nothing, and gave the police the employee's file. This gave them all of the information they were asking for such as his name, address, and other pertinent information. I also had to go through the hassle of putting a stop payment on the check through the company's bank, as Randy did not want him to cash it. Theft or not, he had worked the hours and was legally entitled to the money, but this was beyond Randy. He had gone from our office directly to a check-cashing center, however, and a few weeks later we were notified that we now owed the money to them, money that was of course never paid.

This was my first real inclination of how Randy and Shane dealt with employee relations. They bullied employees, holding their checks for days or weeks at a time, until it was convenient for them to hold a meeting. Their reasoning was as sharp as butter, and I lost count of how many of my colleagues they did this to throughout the course of my employment. Obviously, this was illegal, and several employees had to go as far as contacting the state labor board to be paid what they were owed for hours put in. Cutting corners seemed to be what Randy and Shane were the best at, and they showed it in even the simplest interactions. The most common culprit was in the general manager's payroll. They thought up silly reasons to take large amounts from manager's paychecks, though spoke the gospel of their pay plan as if it were genius.

On one particular week, Dylan, a manager who had worked for over fifty hours received a check for $64.00, after all of the unnecessary fines were applied. There were many occasions when managers found they were making $5 or below hourly after doing their own calculations, and obviously, this was also illegal for un-tipped workers in Wisconsin. Most managers worked at least 50 hours in a week, and Dylan was obviously upset when he saw the amount of his paycheck. Following this, he asked me to give him copies of his paycheck stubs, since he hadn't kept a few of them. In Wisconsin, an employer is legally obligated to give their employees any personnel file information that they request with no questions asked. When the employee asked for copies of the check stubs, I obliged and gave them to him late in my workday near the middle of October. Unfortunately for me, Randy came upstairs in the midst of Dylan's visit. Thinking on my feet, I printed some box topper flyers for his store and put the check stubs at the bottom, though was foiled because he had told Randy that he had come in to pick up his check stub copies, which Randy wasn't aware of. After Dylan left, Randy screamed at me and told me that nothing of that nature was to happen in the future without his approval, because he knew that Dylan was planning to go to the state's labor board with the information. I stood up for myself and told him that as Dylan's employer, we are legally obligated to give him any information he requests. I also told him that was going to stick to the law over what he had to say. Randy was obviously displeased with the fact that I was not following his directions, but I wasn't about to get embroiled in the shoddy business practices he chose to enact along with Shane. They were like the dream team of nightmare employers.

One thing that I did not want my name associated with was the practices that Shane and Randy utilized when dealing with store employees. I did not want to be involved with police earlier in the month, and I did not want to be held responsible for the refusal of the release of Dylan's payroll information. This was a job to me, and I never wanted to do anything that could negatively affect me either at work or personally. Early on, I resolved to be an ally to our store employees because Randy and Shane were both insane. The employees had to have someone on their side, and I intended to be that person. Whether it was giving them their personnel files under the table or double-checking to make sure I had the correct information in their files, I had to be protective. I prided myself on it, and everyone appreciated it – some employees even calling me randomly to ask me how my day was going and if they could send a meal up to the office in appreciation for my hard work, though I always declined. From the day I started to my last day, I continued to be that ally and would not resign the relationships I built for anything, or anyone else.

Among other things, the end of October brought my six-month review. I requested a three-month review after seeing how much work I was doing in comparison to how I was being paid, and the idea had been vetoed. I was making just $12 hourly, routinely worked 5 hours or more a week of overtime (which I was never paid for), and ran countless weekly errands without being paid a dime for mileage. It was difficult for me to take care of my rent much less some backlogged debt, and I believed that I was worth quite a bit more than what I was making. I told Randy this and constantly made reference to the fact that I was barely scraping by. It fell on deaf ears. In his defense, he had given me health insurance within my first month instead of making me wait three due to my need for medication, but health insurance doesn't pay the bills.

Randy requested that my review take place outside of the office (likely so Ralph wouldn't hear anything), and offered to take me to lunch. I accepted, and when he was a half hour late, I expected it. He was paying, after all, and I had to run on his schedule or nothing. We arrived at the restaurant and it felt more like I was reviewing his work instead of the other way around. He asked how I felt about the job and the people, and what things I would change about him and the way he does things. He told me that he trusted me and appreciated me, and that was a big thing because I had gotten very good at hiding my distaste for my work environment. Throughout lunch, he was on his iPhone, and was apparently doing it to calculate my total raise. He gave me a twenty percent increase, which was unheard of for him. I had only been expecting fifty cents if anything, but he reiterated the fact that I had made myself indispensable, and even called Helen incompetent in comparison.

I also said that I would be open to doing some marketing, and even work in stores to get a feel for that side of the business as well. Surprised, he wondered out loud why I would want to do that. I told him that I really wanted to know what it would be like to be on the other side of things. It would be a good way to build relationships with the stores I wasn't so familiar with, as my idea was to work at a different store each month. It would also be a way to make a mess out of some pizza ingredients, no matter how silly it seemed. He agreed and told me that he had thought of me taking on some more marketing duties so we weren't relying so heavily on our paid advertising. He also wanted me to re-vamp our office and make it a bit more 'homey'. He wanted to paint and get pictures to hang on the walls of the cold, echo-laden space, painting me a mental picture of what he expected. I did not mind this whatsoever, mostly since getting creative with other people's money is much better than spending your own.

All in all, I was satisfied with how my review went. I received a raise I wasn't expecting which totaled $2.40 an hour, was looking forward to taking in an additional hundred dollars weekly, and was also looking forward to some new responsibility and getting my feet wet in unfamiliar waters. One thing that was constant with Randy, however, was the fact that he said one thing and did the opposite.

After my review, nothing was ever brought up about either marketing or working in the stores. No matter how many times I asked or reminded him about what we'd discussed, nothing fazed him or got through to him. Eventually, I gave up and forgot about the whole thing. Looked like the only marketing I would get to do would be to make thousands of copies of box topper menus for the stores, which I had been doing all along. If this review was any indication, all this job seemed to be worth was disappointment and aggravation. I got through each day at this point by just wondering what would happen next.

NOVEMBER 2008

November always brings things to get excited about. Whether it is the impending holidays or the fleeting thoughts of a new year on the horizon, it never fails to bring a smile to my face. Life outside of work stayed consistently fine, complete with another successful Halloween recovery. My only complaint was increasing numbers of phone calls and text messages from Randy just wanting to hang out at completely random hours of each and every day. I neglected to take him up on all of these offers, no matter how desperate he seemed. He was my boss and I was still an hourly employee, so I had no obligation to. Shane, on the other hand, seemed to be on the hook with Randy for a 24-hour-a-day job. You never saw Randy without him those days, and it was raising questions from not only the office staff, but from store employees.

Midway through the first complete week of November, I heard screaming that reverberated throughout the walls of our office. The building itself was quiet during the day since hardly anyone was home, and to be honest, the yelling was scary. It felt like I was an innocent bystander to an awful episode of Cops downstairs. It didn't last a few minutes, either – it was about a half hour of near constant screaming.

It was Randy screaming at Shane.

In an after-hours phone call later in the week, Randy told me that he had accidentally picked up the incorrect iPhone (their phones were identical – they even went out and got matching cases, so there was no way to tell them apart) and found something he hadn't been expecting. Not only was it not his phone, but there was a text message on the screen from Nicki, a female general manager. It thanked Shane for the sex the night before and alluded to the fact that it had been happening for awhile. This sent Randy into an utter and complete rage, and the screaming I had heard days before had been from him.

Now, not only was Shane a thief and capable of killing someone and coming to work the next day, he had no issue with sleeping with a store manager while being her direct supervisor.

As it related to Nicki, I wasn't surprised. There had been rumors in the past of not only her sleeping with her assistant managers, but also using drugs and drinking in her store during business hours. Each and every time she was caught, she never received more than a written warning. Most of the offenses would have merited immediate termination at any company but this one. Because, in her words, 'Randy treated her like a daughter', so she got away with all of it unscathed. Every company had to have their token tramp, and it looked like she was ours.

It was in the same phone call that Randy confessed to me once again that he was in love with Shane. This was the reason he hadn't prosecuted him for embezzlement, and was the reason that he had kept the car accident a secret. Instead of full prosecution, Randy paid upwards of five thousand dollars to his lawyer to draft a payback plan, instead of putting him in jail. It was the reason that Shane got away with treating the employees the way he did, and it was the reason why they were spending so much time together. Suppressing my gag reflex, I realized this was over my head. Why would anyone give such an awful person so much leeway? He obviously wasn't getting anything in return, as most of his phone calls to me after hours were asking what he was doing wrong with the situation and essentially 'how he could make Shane love him'.

More and more, I wondered if this job wasn't just a joke that everyone else was in on but me. There was nothing sane happening here, and that was proven beyond the shadow of a doubt each day when I got in deeper. It felt like I could not come in and not have a soap opera-worthy day. All of this from a company whose job it was to make pizza. It was something I never expected. From the company's employees to the constant drama, it seemed like pizza was the last thing on anybody's mind.

While I thought I could get through a week without something dramatic happening, the universe had other plans. In my office one morning early the next week, I heard Ralph shuffling around as usual, but Randy called and asked to speak with him. Forwarding the call, I soon heard not only shuffling, but Ralph screaming at Randy. Instead of getting up and going back to see what was wrong, I closed my office door and opted to go back and ask what was going on after the phone was unceremoniously slammed down.

One thing that Randy never understood was why the company never had money. If we had a good day or a good weekend, he believed that all of our bills would be paid (the total payables being in upwards of $250,000). Since we were a franchise, we had thousands of dollars automatically debited from our bank accounts by the corporate side of the business weekly. These dollars went to the store's food orders as well as advertising and other supplies. Besides this, we dealt with an outside contractor for our direct mail marketing and we paid them nearly $20,000 weekly. By the time we were finished paying both the direct debits and the large advertising cost, we were bone dry, if not overdrawn. Randy did not understand this fact, and constantly called to berate Ralph, figuring it was our accounting doing a bad job at keeping things straight. When Ralph explained this to me, it made sense. I wondered how it didn't make sense to Randy. If there was no money to begin with, why spend what little we did have on high-ticket advertising? We constantly got offers from non-profit organizations and small companies about doing advertising for much cheaper if not free, but these offers were always ignored and put on the back burner. Randy's business sense didn't make any sense to me, and Ralph was left with the same feeling.

Wherever the issues were, they were not with Ralph. He had years of experience in accounting for food businesses, and had even been the person who uncovered Shane's theft. He may have been slow in appearance, but he knew what he was doing and Randy constantly talked down to him and tried to make him feel incompetent. It never worked. Instead of taking it, Ralph would yell right back, disrupting the typical quiet of our office, but standing up for himself. He was the only person who I would ever see stand up to Randy. He always told me that I should do the same, instead of fielding phone calls at all hours of the night and living up to my 'office princess' nickname. The only issue there was I didn't know how to push back without completely screwing myself over. When you upset Randy, there was no redemption... unless your name was Shane. Everyone that I had ever seen cause problems had either been terminated for a ridiculous reason, or just quit and was never heard from again. Clearly, this wouldn't happen from either Ralph or myself, so we would both have to grin and bear it.

Imagine my surprise when I went through a full week in the office without something ridiculous happening. On a weekly trip to our franchise store that serviced my home address for a quick dinner, an assistant manager I interacted with often asked me a question.

"Where were you on Saturday? We had a lot of fun without you!"

"What was Saturday?"

"We cleaned out the Germantown store."

The Germantown store was located about fifteen minutes outside of the Milwaukee area, and seemed to do pretty well on a weekly basis while it was open. It came as a surprise to me when Randy announced to me before payroll one Monday afternoon in July that he was closing the store, and that it would be effective the day after the announcement. Hesitantly, I wrote up a letter to attach to the employee's paychecks, and Randy assured me that he and Shane would take care of the rest.

Seemed like they did a bang-up job.

From the constant calls from vendors wanting to pick up their product and rented machines to still paying rent for months after the closing, I wondered what he meant by 'cleaned out', and was almost afraid to ask.

"Randy and Shane called me on Saturday and told me I had to go to the Germantown store and help them clean it out."

"What did that entail?"

"Oh, there were maggots in the make table with spoiled food both there and in the walk-in cooler. It was myself, Randy, Shane and a handful of other managers."

I stopped him. I was fully convinced I was about to puke in my mouth.

From the remainder of his story, I gathered that about five people assisted in cleaning out our former store space at the behest of the landlord who wanted to be able to re-rent the property. Randy sat on a bucket on his laptop the entire time, and everyone else cleaned. Everything had been a mess, and it seemed that it would all be a loss. Not to these guys. They salvaged what they could of the food and supplies that had not spoiled and brought it into other stores. This absolutely, positively astounded me. This store had closed almost six months prior, and they were honestly going to attempt to use six-month-old food in our other franchise stores. The supplies didn't bother me so much – paper products could not really spoil, but the food? It disgusted me. When he told me that, I made sure to ask him if any of the food had been brought to his store, and he shook his head. I emitted a sigh of relief, but was still second-guessing myself as I delved into the pizza I brought home for dinner that night. The only other alarming part to me was that Randy just sat there and 'supervised' while everyone else got their hands dirty and fought back the urge to vomit at what I'm sure was an awful sight. How could I work for someone like that? How did the man get any sleep at all? If I would have been in his shoes, I would have been elbow deep in spoiled food and maggots, just showing that I was not at all superior. It would have been an attempt to make up for what had happened. Not Randy. He could not be bothered to do anything but sit on his plastic bucket and obsessively check his e-mail. Important people don't have time for a simple thing like taking responsibility for their actions.

Up until this point, Randy and Shane's interaction with the store employees hadn't affected me at all. It left a sour taste in my mouth to know that I had a hand in cutting the paychecks that were less than what many teenagers make working minimum wage, but nothing they did to the employees had directly affected me. I always heard about the things they did from other people, but reality had never come to slap me in the face until then.

It was obvious that Randy and Shane never followed typical practices when it came down to employees. Shortly before the Thanksgiving holiday, there had been an issue between a shift manager and a driver at one of our stores. This store was in an unfortunate area of town, with a lot of gang activity and other crime commonplace. Before hiring each employee, we ran a background check and if there were infractions such as gang related activity or theft we typically looked at other applicants first. Randy and Shane cared if it was some form of sexual crime (especially toward a child), but otherwise it seemed as if we were saturated with former gang members and thieves. Considering there was a thief helping to run the place, it obviously was not too tall an order.

There was a rift between the shift manager, Dennis, and a delivery driver at the store in question, with the delivery driver threatening bodily harm against Dennis, saying he would 'bring his boys around after his shift'. Once Dennis alerted Randy and Shane to the possibility, there was a meeting called at the office with both of them, at the exact same time. What Randy and Shane were thinking doing that was completely beyond me. Dennis showed up alone, but the driver showed up with no fewer than three people who had nothing to do with the situation. For shits and giggles, I looked the driver's background up one more time: it was saturated with weapon possession, drug charges, and other gang-related crimes.

It only took about five minutes of sitting next to one another before a screaming verbal argument broke out. I was sitting in my office and I overheard, and Randy and Shane were in the conference room unpacking and applying their new matching iPhone cases. I glanced into the waiting area, and the driver was standing up with his friends surrounding him, and I knew that this would escalate and it would escalate fast. Instead of getting involved myself, I ran to the conference room and opened the door without knocking.

"You two need to go out to the waiting room and do something about this. They are screaming at each other and a fight is going to start."

The prospect of an all-out fight was the only thing that would get Shane out of his seat at that point, and he accompanied me back to my office and took the two men into the conference room. This left the driver's 'friends' out in the waiting room, who constantly came to my door and asked everything from if they could have a soda from the refrigerator to where the restroom was. There wasn't any further arguing or yelling that I could hear. When all was said and done and the meeting was over, I went to the refrigerator to grab my lunch leftovers and found that all of the remaining soda had been taken, when I knew there were at least four in there previously. Not only had a physical altercation almost broken out in my office; the driver's friends had stolen the remaining soda out of our refrigerator. Some people truly have no shame.

I got through the remainder of the day and even the following Monday without so much as a peep from Dennis, Randy or Shane about what had happened. Monday afternoon at 5:30 PM, there was a knock at the front door of the office. As a safety practice, I locked the door after Ralph left at 5:00, because I was the only one in the office and sometimes I could not hear the door open. The knock surprised me, because on Mondays Randy and Shane were gone to their weekly manager meeting across town, and I wasn't expecting anyone.

Behind the door was the driver from the meeting the week before, with no fewer than five other individuals. I let them in.

"What can I help you with?"

"I'm supposed to be meeting with Shane."

"Shane isn't here, he is at our manager's meeting."

"Why the fuck would he fuckin' tell me to come here? Where is he?"

"I don't know why he would tell you to come here, but he isn't here."

He and his friends continued to get closer and closer to me, and knowing what he had done in the past I had red flags flying in my head. At one point, he was about four inches from my face.

"You don't need to be a bitch about it, we'll just wait for him!" When had I been a bitch?

"I apologize if what I said was taken that way, but just have a seat and let me call him."

"Fuck. Fine." He and his friends sat down on the couch, and I headed into my office confidently, closing and locking the door behind myself. I hadn't shown fear to their faces, because I felt that they might have reacted like a shark to blood.

Picking up the phone, I dialed Randy's number. Voicemail. Dialed Shane's number. Voicemail. I did this over and over about six times before I got a phone call back from Randy.

"The driver you guys met with on Friday is here, and he just got in my face and yelled at me because he was supposed to be meeting with you and Shane."

"They were told that the meeting was here at the store. You need to tell them to come here."

"Randy, I'm afraid. I'm here by myself and I just had five people in my face."

"Just tell them to come here." Click.

Staring at the phone with my heart still beating a mile a minute, I took a few seconds to get my bearings before going back out to the waiting area.

"I just spoke to Randy, and he said that your meeting is at the former office, where they have their meetings."

"Those motherfuckers didn't tell us that, they told us to come here!"

"I'm sorry, but they aren't here. I am the only person here. I was instructed to tell you to go there."

The six men turned around and left without another word. As soon as they were out of view of the peephole, I locked the door and proceeded to pack my things and leave. I didn't care what time it was, I didn't care that I was supposed to leave in a half hour. I just needed to leave. I was scared out of my mind.

Later that night, I was out at a concert with friends when Randy called me.

"Did you leave early today?"

"Yes."

"Why would you do that, Liz?"

"Because I was scared after I had six people screaming at me because someone didn't tell them where their meeting was."

"You should have told me."

"I did tell you. I called you and Shane five times each before someone picked up. I was locked in my office when I spoke to you before because I was afraid."

"I don't understand why you would be afraid. Tell me what happened."

Instead of getting into an argument, I recounted the events that had happened, and the only one that stuck out to Randy was that I locked the door after Ralph left.

"Why do you lock the door?"

"Because at that point in the day, I don't have meetings and I am in the office by myself."

"I don't want you to lock the door anymore. If anything like that happens again, Shane and I are right downstairs."

I honestly laughed out loud. By time either of them actually got up the single floor, I would be seriously injured or dead. I knew what the men who had been at the office were capable of, and it wasn't knitting sweaters and stuffing teddy bears. The resolution that I received was being able to take off half of the next day, since I had friends visiting from Illinois. It still astounded me that Randy did not understand the reason for my being upset. I am not a helpless woman by any means, but when there are six people screaming in my face and I'm alone, I am not about to tempt fate.

At this point, Randy had put me in immediate danger. He didn't think that anything would have happened, but I was convinced something would have. If it had, I would have been helpless and alone. I was as polite as I could be to those guys, and they were still up in my face like I had made a bad 'your mom' joke.

This should have been the end of everything for me. I should have just quit and filed unemployment claiming I was in a hostile work environment. Instead of that, I stuck around. I continued to lock the door after Ralph left every day, just didn't mention it, and everything went back to normal. I don't know exactly what could be considered 'normal' in a situation like this, but it was better than being maimed or murdered by former employees just because I went into work on Monday morning.

DECEMBER 2008

As if November's events hadn't been enough, December was insane right out of the proverbial gates. While I should have been planning my twenty-third birthday party and getting excited about seeing family later in the month, I was busy dealing with some of the most intense stress I had ever experienced.

Each week on Friday, Ralph and I were to clean the office. This included me sweeping and vacuuming, as well as mopping if necessary, every room in the office, and Ralph sweeping his office and taking care of the trash in the bathroom. Taking out the trash and wiping down bathroom mirrors and countertops was also on the list of things to do. Instead of employing a part-time cleaning person, as the accountant and office manager, we were also required to clean toilets. It wasn't fair, but I took it as more normal duties and even looked forward to it. There was something in cleaning that had a stress-relieving quality, and after the weeks I had been having, I could use any relief I could get. At the end of December's first week, Randy had decided that it was not good enough.

The main restroom in the office was located in the hallway, and there was a second one in the conference room, which Randy typically used. Ralph and I split the task of cleaning the main one, and there had never been an ill word spoken of its' cleanliness. I was surprised to find the door locked one morning, and imagined that it was a mistake. Taking the initiative, I called the building's maintenance supervisor and stated that I'd come in to find the bathroom door locked. He came upstairs and unlocked it, knowing too well how Randy could be, since he was always calling him to do the most asinine tasks. These tasks included but were not limited to: regluing laminate onto his kitchen counter, changing the magnets in his closet doors, waxing his floors once a week free (instead of paying the $75 fee), and the list goes on and on. Suffice to say that he was annoyed with Randy, and that wasn't a surprise. Once I got into the bathroom, I saw that someone had pulled the bag from the trashcan and thrown dirty paper towels all over the floor. Since Ralph obviously would not do this and I certainly hadn't, Randy was my only other choice. Since he knew that that bathroom was the one that Ralph dealt with weekly, I was sure that it was nothing more than Randy just making more jabs at Ralph. He had been trying to chase him out of his job for at least four months, and it was clear he was going to continue to get more and more petty.

During a typical phone call with Randy, I mentioned that I had had the bathroom door unlocked.

"Why did you do that? I locked it."

"Why?"

"It was dirty."

"We just cleaned it, Randy."

"It was dirty."

There was no use fighting it. I was working for a child. How could we clean the bathroom if the door was locked? Why not take initiative and say, 'hey, could you double-check the bathroom?' A polite approach was obviously too much to ask. Acting like a seven year old who didn't get his mint chocolate chip ice cream at the grocery store is a *much* better plan. This also told me that he had been the person to remove the trash bag from its container and throw the dirty paper towels all over the floor. This had to be something for America's Funniest Home Videos. There was no way this was actually my life.

As they say, there is no rest for the wicked. And in this case, it was obvious that Randy and Shane weren't getting much, since each day brought a new challenge to the table. Only one day after the bathroom-locking debacle, I found myself in a late meeting with Randy, Shane, and Ralph, where I was informed that I would be learning Ralph's job. Randy's initial excuse was that he 'wanted me to be able to do it in case of a vacation', but I knew exactly what his plans were as soon as the words left his lips. Ralph had recently turned sixty and because of that, his health insurance premium had doubled. Randy always made reference to it in casual conversation, but I didn't think that he would go so far as to completely push Ralph out of a job. With that, he would open himself to a firestorm, including the possibility of an unemployment claim at least, an age discrimination suit at worst. Knowing Ralph, he would go for all of it. Picking up the mechanics of accounting would not be difficult, but I didn't have the knowledge for dealing with the financials of an eight million dollar a year company. I took accounting courses at both the high school and college level, and barely retained any of the information. I had never dealt with QuickBooks, the company's accounting software, and I was rusty, to say the least. This led me to go to the library and check out copies of both *Accounting for Dummies* and *Bookkeeping for Dummies*, because every little bit helps! At least that's what they say.

After this meeting, Ralph thought that I was in with Randy on whatever was happening. He treated me differently, was incredibly short and snarky with responses to questions, and never talked to me about Randy anymore. On one hand, I was thankful, but on the other hand I was angry. I didn't want Ralph to think that I was in cahoots with Randy, or in any way attempting to chase him out of a job. I never wanted to be an accountant. I didn't have the training or desire to work with numbers, when mathematics has never been my strong suit. Sure, Ralph may have been a negative person, but he was companionship for my long days, and he really did know what he was doing. I could not predict how this would end, but I didn't imagine it would be good.

After the initial meeting, nothing about the new responsibilities was mentioned. Randy wanted me to spend time with Ralph each week to begin learning everything, especially before his upcoming vacation, and we were asked to write up a plan for the remainder of training. As someone who picks new things up relatively quickly, the first few training sessions were a breeze. Like Helen, though, Ralph got upset when I clicked too fast on the computer or when I did things differently than he was used to. It wasn't difficult to learn once I got started. I was asked to take care of Ralph's responsibilities while he was gone on a week's vacation, and was confused as to how I was going to do that with my own things to take care of. I said that I would try, but made no promises. I spent a couple of hours a day with Ralph the week before he left, and was confident that I would be able to hammer it down for the next week. I had taken enough notes that there were no problems in sight.

My confidence extended to the rest of the week. I was brought out to a birthday lunch at Benihana with Randy and Shane, one not including Ralph on purpose. I was called and taken off guard while I was headed out for lunch by myself, but appreciated the gesture. They even gave me a humorously unintended gift: Shane split his pants trying to carry two cases of copy paper at once. After lunch, I found out that Shane had purchased a small cake for me, with a Batman candle on the top, since he knew I was excited about the new film's DVD release. Something still seemed fishy. While I appreciated that my birthday was being recognized, it felt awful to know that they hadn't included Ralph on purpose; they hadn't even purchased a cake large enough for four. Ralph shrugged it off, though, saying that he would bring me out to lunch when he got back from his vacation. When I left on Friday, Batman candle in hand, I was looking forward to not only my 'Third Annual 21st Birthday Party', but a week without the negative energy that was Ralph and his complaints about anything and everything, although the lunch was a nice gesture. With the newest development of not being invited to my birthday lunch, it was clear that Ralph wasn't just negative at this point… he was straight up pissed. I understood his frustration. Nobody likes to be left out of things, especially things that the entire office should have been involved in.

Ralph was still convinced that I was involved in Randy's decision to train me on his job. After the first meeting, he treated me completely differently, until one day before his vacation when I entered his office and asked him what the issues were.

"You think I had something to do with this whole job thing, don't you?"

"What do you mean?"

"You've been treating me completely differently, Ralph. Like I'm somehow in on it."

"Well, are you?"

"Why would I want to do your job? I have enough to deal with."

"I guess…"

"I don't have the experience to do what you do, and I don't want to. I'm not in on anything. I don't want to learn."

From that conversation, things seemed to get better. Ralph was starting new conversations with me on everything from typical work banter to asking if I watched any *Dancing With the Stars*. I suggested movies for him to watch, even borrowing him a few titles. It seemed to be back the way it was before Randy's decision came down. We were not best friends by any means, but we still tolerated one another and it was nice to have someone to talk to. Before then he hadn't been speaking to me at all, spare niceties of 'good morning's and 'goodnight's.

It was all undue stress that I didn't need.

At my birthday party that Saturday night, I drank an entire bottle of Cook's champagne on my own, which led to me attempting to take naps every twenty minutes, until one of my friends found me and made me wake up. It had been a nice way to forget about everything that was going on at work. There wasn't any crazy drama, it was just friends drinking and having a good time. I missed the times when nights like that weren't so few and far between. The party finally ended at around 3 AM, when I passed out on our loveseat. When my phone started to ring at 7 AM, I hit 'ignore' almost as fast as I heard the sound of my ring tone. After hitting 'ignore', I didn't expect to hear it go off again. Setting it down and rolling back over, it started to ring again. Figuring that it was my parents, I answered the phone without looking at its' caller ID, obviously still drunk from the night before.

"Hello?"

"Liz, it's Shane."

"How can I help you?" I asked in a sarcastic voice, looking over at the clock and seeing that yes, it was seven in the fucking morning on a Saturday.

"Liz, I need your computer password."

"Why?"

"I need it."

Not wanting to fight because sleep was far more important, I gave him the password and hung up no sooner than the words left my lips.

They had to be planning something. There was no doubt in my mind that Shane calling me at 7 AM on a Saturday had to be an indication of their next hackneyed plan going into action, but I had no idea what that plan consisted of. I hadn't taken much time to think about it, passing out almost as soon as I took the call. I remembered as soon as I woke up, however, checking my text messages and voicemails as most technologically obsessed people do. There had been an irritated-sounding message from Shane from his first call, asking for my computer password, and the other missed calls made it obvious that he had been trying to get a hold of me since before 7, even. I was not upset that they had tried to get a hold of me, actually. I was upset because they knew that my birthday party had been the night before, and knew that I would likely not be awake. On Saturdays, I sleep in until noon or two PM, on some occasions. The fact that I was not awake at 7 AM should not have been a surprise. As an hourly employee, I had no incentive to even picking up the phone call, except for not having to deal with a line of questioning on Monday morning. One thing that this party had taught me was that I had friends who actually didn't work in this cesspool of a company, and for that I was thankful. They gave me a sweet escape from the chaos and unbelievable nature of my weekday life. Now, the chaos was seeping its' way into my weekends, and this was war.

Winters in Wisconsin can be brutal. They start off like a mouse and finish like a lion… about six months later. For the last few years, we haven't seen much show until Christmas or after, and it lasts all the way until April on a bad year. This year, luck seemed to be on our side because yes, we were going to have a white Christmas. The chances of anyone getting to work before the incoming Christmas break, however, were slim to none. On the Friday of Ralph's vacation week, there was a snowfall of two feet overnight. When I woke up to go to work, I shuffled around the house and started to get ready before checking my phone, being greeted by a text message from my landlord.

"If you don't have to go out today, don't. Will be by this afternoon."

This piqued my interest, and I headed to the front window to survey the damage. There was over two feet of snow on our front balcony, on the sidewalks, and on the driveway. The cars unfortunate enough to be parked on the street were almost completely covered in snow. One look outside, and I said a big 'no' to going to work. I both called and texted Randy, telling him that there was no way I was going to get out of the driveway, much less to work without killing myself and/or other drivers on the road. I had never called in sick a day within my almost nine month tenure, and I figured that a storm I coined 'Winter Storm Bullshit' would be as good a reason as any. It was 7:30 AM besides – who wouldn't love a few more hours of sleep?

After doing the deed, I climbed back into bed and woke up again at 11:00 AM to a text message from Randy asking if I could get in by 1:00. Begrudgingly, I said I would try – only because I knew that the snowplowing in the City of Milwaukee was done before the snow was finished falling in many cases, and perhaps if I went through town I would get to work alive.

An incredibly tall order this would be.

By this point, my roommate was awake, and for some reason also had to go to work. We attempted to put on happy faces as we went outside to survey what we were working with, and I grabbed the shovel from our basement, and he grabbed the snow blower. This wasn't just any snow blower – it looked as if it was from the 1970's or before, and there was quite a bit of trouble getting it to work in snow that was any higher than six inches. I jumped from our back door into our driveway, and was buried in snow up to the middle of my thighs. We worked for almost two hours on snow blowing and shoveling ourselves halfway out of the driveway, and finally our landlord showed up with his brand new snow blower, impressed we'd gotten as far as we had. After he arrived, it took about 20 minutes before we were able to pull our cars out, and I somehow arrived to work in one piece by 2:00 PM.

Really, there was no reason for me to be there. None of our vendors were open, as it had been declared a snow emergency, and the only thing that I had to finish for the week was payroll. It would have taken me around twenty minutes, but instead I worked from 2:00 PM until 8:00 PM, and finally packed it in to leave when Randy and Shane made themselves known. Neither of them said a word to me or thanked me for braving the rough weather to come in, and it was at that point I understood where I must have been on their ladder of importance. As long as they had their paychecks, right?

Shane's urgency in getting my computer password was made completely obvious when I returned to work the following Monday. I walked into my office to a completely different computer setup, and Ralph whining about how he could not get onto his computer. Before surveying the damage in my office, I headed into his, where he sat staring blank-faced at his Windows login screen, because his password had been reset and he had no idea what it was. Going into my own office, I saw that my tower computer had been replaced with a laptop and some form of docking device, and turned it on cautiously before seeing just how severe it was. I didn't know my password, either. Ralph had been sitting in front of his computer for almost an hour, trying to figure out what his password could have been changed to. This had to have been some form of test. I picked up the phone and tried to call both Randy and Shane, which Ralph had already done, and neither of them picked up. It looked like the day was going to be incredibly fulfilling, staring at the blue Windows login screen like it would tell me what the answer was. And when you asked for a password hint, all it gave you was the word 'pizza'. Some hint, guys.

By time they finally got back to us a half hour later via phone, they seemed surprised that I would not have been able to guess the password.

The password was p8ssw0rd. A frickin' genius could not have guessed that password, and giving a hint like 'pizza' really wasn't much of one.

When both Ralph and I logged into our computers to try and re-acclimate ourselves, we found that they had cleared out Ralph's hard drive but replaced his files. I wasn't so lucky. All of my files were gone; from the weekly reports I was responsible for to the resume I kept just in case I needed it. I had to call them again.

"Oh, there's a jump drive there, with all your files on it."

"Where is it?"

"It's not there? I wonder where it could be."

Twenty minutes later, Shane came upstairs in a chipper mood as ever, holding out the jump drive in the palm of his hand.

"You asked for this?' He spoke with a shit-eating grin.

"Yeah, thanks." I replied in an annoyed tone.

And off he went: back down the elevator into Randy's office. A lap dog just looking for his pat on the head for a job well done.

Pinpointing exactly where my distaste for Shane came in is difficult. Nothing he had done had directly affected me. One thing that I can say is that for someone who was only five years older than me, he certainly acted with an air of superiority that drove me crazy. He constantly talked down to me, second-guessed me, and made me feel like I was an inch tall. Even if it was over something that I was proficient at, his monotonous tone and line of questioning was irritating at best. It got to a point where I didn't know if he was my boss or if Randy was. It seemed like if Randy needed something, he would send Shane or have Shane call me. To say that it was childish would be a disservice. Randy knew how I felt about him from the point he'd confided in me about everything, and still pressed on.

Through my own research, it was obvious that it was the office manager's job to organize the company's yearly Christmas party. The year before, it had been held at a piano bar, and the year before that the managers and administrative staff had gone to see a theater production. When I questioned Randy as to what he wanted to do this year, he could not give me a straight answer regarding either catering something or going out. One thing that I knew I wanted to do was organize a Secret Santa gift exchange. Through speaking to Ralph, I knew that it was something that had never been done. During my weekly trip to the general manager's meeting, I informed the staff of my plan for a Secret Santa exchange, and had any interested parties put their names in and listed what they would like within the given criteria. The gifts themselves would be simple - nothing over twenty dollars and nothing extravagant. Many of the managers asked for simple things like cigarettes, DVDs, or gas gift cards. The exchange itself would take place at the party.

Since Randy had given me no indication as to wanting to go out, I worked with Jake, the office's property manager, and rented out the building's community room for the festivities. I told Randy of what I had done and he stated that we would have dinner catered in, perhaps watch a Christmas film and that would be that. When asking what he should have catered in, I suggested everything from sandwiches to a burrito bar, and he gave me no inclination as to his decision until the night of the party.

He and Shane had gone to a local Famous Dave's and purchased the food there, coming in with several trays of food forty-five minutes after the party began. I had been left to deal with everyone coming in, and nothing had been set up the way it was supposed to be. Though I had previously asked if I needed to do anything but be there, Randy always said no. As soon as he arrived, though, I was told to purchase several cases of soda and a bag of ice, which meant that I got to leave and come back to the party that I had planned. When I got back, the trays were put out, but all of the food was cold and our employees were putting their plates together and putting the plates in the microwave to warm them. Classy.

Instead of sitting around and getting angry, I proceeded to drink one whiskey and coke after another to blot out any memories of this party for the future. Randy and Shane purchased a bottle of Patron for the festivities, and the only family-like atmosphere the party possessed was when everyone toasted with their shots of tequila.

The Secret Santa exchange was a disaster. Everyone picked names, and if they didn't get someone they particularly liked wound up leaving their names and gifts on their tables when leaving. This meant that I got to buy three Secret Santa gifts, whereas everyone else got to buy one.

Not even our Christmas party could be decent.

Christmas itself came and went, and endearing thoughts of a new year and new possibilities were within reach. I had purchased both Randy and Shane each a gift certificate for a haircut at Randy's favorite salon, and was thanked with hugs and endearing words about what perfect gifts they were. I didn't know what was going to happen with Ralph or this new job I was learning, but one thing that I did know was that I was happy to say goodbye to 2008 and hello to 2009. The day before the New Year's break, I was called into a meeting in Randy's apartment shortly before I was to leave for the day. The topic was strange: Shane and the dress code.

From the beginning of my employment to the present, I always stuck to a business casual dress code. Dress pants, sweaters, and button-down shirts. I would sneak in a pair of black jeans once and awhile, but for the most part I stuck to my understanding of 'business casual' to a T. Randy's new idea for pushing Ralph over the edge was going to be to require the office staff to wear the store manager's uniforms. A hunter green polo shirt, khaki pants, and either a visor or a hat bearing the franchise's name.

The store manager's uniform. Hat or visor included. To work in an office.

Just the thought of this infuriated me. I chose to work in administrative positions so that I wouldn't have to wear cheaply made polo shirts with a restaurant's name printed on them. And I sure as hell wasn't about to wear a visor just because Randy didn't like the fact that Ralph had to wear Velcro shoes and only had so many choices when it came to clothing. He wore a size 4XL shirt if not larger, and never wore anything outside the guidelines. The fact of the matter was that Randy just didn't like him, and wanted to figure out a surefire way to get him out.

"I am not going to wear a store manager's uniform."

"Why not? It would be comfortable."

"It would be humiliating, Randy."

"Why is that? Does working here humiliate you?"

"No. Having to sit behind my desk and wear a visor and a manager's uniform would."

He didn't understand. And then, the topic switched to Shane. I started this conversation.

"Randy, who is my boss?"

"What do you mean?"

"Just what I asked. Who is my boss?"

"I am."

"Tell Shane that."

This led into a long-winded conversation about the fact that I hated being micromanaged by Shane – or had he had begun being called, the "golden boy" – and I outlined several instances when he did so. Randy could not understand my upset, even though we discussed it for a good twenty minutes and he opted to call Shane into the meeting so that I could confront him to his face. This irritated me, and when I looked up at the clock, I was supposed to be gone over a half hour earlier. At this point, I didn't care anymore, and just wanted to leave.

Shane played dumb, as per usual. He went on about how he never thought the things he said to me were inappropriate or micromanaging, and sweetly told Randy that he would try to deal with me differently in the future. I didn't believe it for a second, but whatever would get me out of that meeting was good enough for me.

No resolution was ever figured out.

No matter what happened at this place, there was never a solid resolution to anything. Thoughts were fleeting, and I was certain that after the meeting – er, confrontation – I'd been backed into with Randy and Shane, things would not be changing for the better anytime soon. At the beginning of the day, I had been daydreaming about what would happen in the year to come. By the end, I was looking forward to nothing but taking about three Tylenol PM's after downing a beer and passing out, drowning in the thoughts of how I'd wasted almost nine months of my life here. There were no longer thoughts of how things would improve, but instead I was battening down the hatches and attempting to imagine how I would get through. I would have rather been struck down by lightning or hit by a bus than go back to work after the weekend was over. Somehow, I had to find the strength to grin and bear it, to put on a happy face and attempt to find a way. Nothing about life is easy without hard work, and I figured that if I continued putting in the work, that karma might have my back.

JANUARY 2009

With the New Year came new headaches. I was spending as much time with Ralph as possible to learn his job relatively quickly, but didn't want my normal responsibilities to suffer. I often put learning on the back burner to take care of everything else – payroll, new hires, customer complaints, and copying marketing materials for the stores to name a few. There just wasn't time within a 40-hour week to donate twelve or more to sitting next to Ralph to learn how to put together his accounting reports and how QuickBooks worked.

While I was home, I often had my nose buried in either *Accounting for Dummies* or *Bookkeeping for Dummies*, and had purchased the workbooks to accompany both. My confidence was not in question; the fact was that I had no business becoming an accountant. I should have been offered the chance to take a formal class to refresh my knowledge at the very least, but it was never brought up. I knew that I possessed the ability to get everything done, but was confused at some things. It would all be worth it so that I would no longer be in the middle of Ralph and Randy's power struggle. Ralph hated his job, and he told me a new reason for it each and every day. I always had store managers asking why I was sticking around, stating that I could do so much better. There was no way for me to find a new job and interview for such with my schedule being monopolized the way that it was.

My work hours were 9 AM to 6 PM, with an hour break for lunch. I rarely left when I was supposed to, often because there were still things to be taken care of and because I didn't want to have missed deadlines or other issues coupled with learning an entirely new job. These hours were never paid, and it became all the more real when I left the office at 8 PM one night. Why was I still doing this? Shouldn't I have been given a choice or at least some warning? I hadn't even been given that, and I feared how far things would go if Ralph did wind up leaving.

With an already stressful workload, I was always irked when a store manager neglected to tell me a new hire was coming in for paperwork, or when someone from a store came in to ask for something without calling first. I always wanted to know what I was going to have to deal with on any given day. It wasn't a surprise when I got one or two new hires a week that didn't have appointments, but it didn't mean I got any less upset.

I had started attending the weekly general manager's meetings and got about ten minutes each week to speak to the managers and tell them what I needed from them, or if there were issues with any of the paperwork they were sending in. It was a good way for the managers to be able to speak face-to-face with at least one member of the office staff, to pose questions to us if they wanted to. For the managers, it was a break from the five to seven hours they spent each Monday being reamed out for mistakes they'd made the week prior. Many of the mistakes weren't a big deal to anyone sane, but to Randy and Shane's control-freak regime, it meant being able to dream up new reasons to dock the manager's pay.

To go through a week without a phone call from an angst-ridden manager would have surprised me. It never happened, and it was only because there were always new reasons for them to be upset. Either Randy and Shane were changing the rules on them *again*, or they had been dealing with surprise visits to their stores and just wanted my advice. Randy hated that I had any dealings with the managers, and did everything that he could to keep me at a safe distance from them. It seemed like he didn't want them to talk to me so that I would never find out the way that things were actually run or the way that people were actually being treated. Any logical person would see that this place was not being run by rocket scientists, but the rumor mill in the stores was running rampant with stories about Randy and Shane, both what they'd been doing to the managers and what was going on behind closed doors.

During one of my conversations, Tim, area-supervisor-turned-store-manager, stated that Randy and Shane had been ordering pizza from his store at anywhere between 1 and 3 AM recently, and that Shane always answered the door. He wasn't dressed to work, though – one driver said that his shirt was un-tucked and his shoes weren't on during one visit, and another said that Shane came to the door in a t-shirt and his boxers during another. They were so clueless. There was no way to prove either instance, but many of the managers had the same reaction as I did: what was going on?

I know that getting involved in the rumor mill and talking to the managers was a bad choice on my part, but it also helped me keep a clearer picture of things going on that I never would have known about otherwise. Without my conversations with these managers, I never would have found out the story of Randy and Shane spending nights together, and I would still be Randy's silent 'princess' who could do no wrong. It wasn't that I wanted to stir up controversy; I had always just wished that Randy were more honest. I wished that he didn't screw people over so much. There were a lot of things I wished, but these wishes were never granted. I never understood why Randy kept everything so secret – what did he have to hide? He had told me more about himself than he had told most people, but why did everything still have to be under lock and key?

Things with Randy and Ralph were souring further and further as the time ticked by. Constant arguments both in meetings and phone calls were commonplace, and it was hard to get through a day without Ralph wanting to talk to me about Randy's newest big ideas for my training. I told Randy that I would not come out a professional right away, but that I would have to learn by doing. Randy, on the other hand, never shared anything with me, even if it directly affected me. All of this added to my stress, and it there was no end in sight. I had a full listing of Ralph's responsibilities and step-by-step instructions, knowing that it would be only a matter of time before he was gone for good.

On a Monday late in the month, Randy and Shane hadn't been able to make enough time to come up the one floor to pick up the payroll, so I was asked to close the office early and bring it to the general manager's meeting. When I got there, I was elated at getting out of work early, but he asked me to stick around for a meeting. This changed my mood significantly, and it was only because no matter what, I knew that I wasn't going to be leaving anytime soon. I sat down at Randy's desk while I waited for the group to come back from a break, still confused as to why I was there. It was no sooner than twenty minutes later that Shane pulled me into a meeting that Randy had nothing to do with.

"One of our managers is concerned about how he was treated in the office last week, Liz."

"Which day was it? Which manager was it? What did he need?"

"Dan said that he came in to get some copies made, and that you were very short with him and that cannot happen in the future."

"Dan did not call first. Everybody knows that if I need to clear my schedule to assist them with something that they need to call first, especially because I'm trying to learn Ralph's job."

"I understand that, but the managers can't have something like this to talk about. Let me bring him in."

Late the week before, Dan, a general manager, had come in near the end of my day with his laptop and copy paper, wanting me to print and copy around a thousand flyers for him. When he popped in without notice, I had two new hires filling out paperwork, and was bouncing from my office to Ralph's doing both my work and continuing to learn Ralph's job. Obviously, I didn't have the time to stop and spend the time it would take to wait for an e-mail to print, and copy Dan's flyers. My priorities were the new hires and wishing that the clock moved about ten times faster than it actually did. When Dan came that afternoon, I *had* been frazzled and short with him – I was annoyed. It was common knowledge that if I was needed, they needed to call first. Dan expected me to drop everything that I was doing in order to help him, when most managers who dropped in to do something like that would have their documents ready for duplication, and would do the copying themselves. Dan didn't want that – he wanted me to do everything for him, and there was had been no time for it.

I explained my case to Shane, and Dan as well when he was pulled in. Dan had a smug answer for everything.

"I understand that she was busy, but she didn't have to treat me that way."

"When I ask you to do something so simple as to call before you come into the office, I don't think it's too much to ask."

"I didn't have access to a phone, and didn't think about it."

"I'm sorry if I upset you, but in the future you should know that if you need me to do something intensive like that for you, that you need to call first."

The confrontation lasted a good twenty minutes, and I spent most of the time wondering what Shane and Randy were expecting to get out of it. Did they want me to have some sort of epic freak-out and storm away? I could see the disappointment on their faces as soon as I left the room unscathed. Why they always wanted to get a rise out of me I would never know, but an off-color comment or joke would have sufficed. It was also during this meeting that I learned that I truly could not trust anyone. Anyone would throw me under the bus, and my trust in my co-workers was dwindling further and further every second.

Two days before February 1st, Randy pulled Ralph into a meeting shortly before he was set to leave. He had called me and told me to ask Ralph to stay, which confused me but which also piqued my interest. Was he trying to get under Ralph's skin again? Was there anything that I had done or said which had caused the meeting to be called? Confident in the second not being the case, I anxiously awaited work the next day to see exactly what had transpired.

"I have one day left!" Ralph stated excitedly as he looked to me while we walked in together the next morning.

"What do you mean?" I asked in utter and complete surprise.

"Tomorrow is my last day. I was almost done yesterday. I wanted to quit, but Randy wanted to make sure you could get every last piece of information you could."

The words echoed in my head all day. How could Randy have made this choice without even asking me if I needed any more time? There was no way I was ready to take on both jobs, and was immediately put into panic mode. While Ralph sat in his office writing personal e-mails and perusing the Web all day, I did the best I could to keep my cool and figure things out on my own, until I got a phone call from Randy.

"Did Ralph tell you?"

"That tomorrow's his last day, yes. I just wish I could have gotten a little bit of warning."

"What more warning would you have needed? You finished the training schedule, I just figured you would be ready."

"What is going to happen with my other responsibilities? How do you expect me to get everything done?"

"I intend to give you another increase effective on February 1st. I also want to bring someone in part-time to help you, because I know you're going to be busy."

"I don't know how I'm going to do it all, Randy."

"You're going to need to find a way."

Now, I not only had to deal with the impending doom of being both the office manager and accountant, but of collecting resumes and holding interviews for a new office assistant position. I was thankful for his realization that I would need help, but was still losing my mind at the fact that the next week I was officially going it alone. I would no longer be able to go back to Ralph's office with questions or just to chat, and knew that I did not have all of the knowledge I would need. That choice wasn't mine, and Randy took it upon himself to make sure that Ralph was gone, and gone quickly.

Interviewing prospective office assistants and finding a good fit would take a lot of time that I didn't have. Randy gave me the freedom to write my own help wanted ad and make my own selections for interviews based on the resumes I'd received. Considering I was informed of my ability to hire an assistant in the last week of January and was expected to have someone ready to go by the first week of February, I wasn't envisioning finding someone to be an easy process.

On principle, I don't get along well with other females. Since most office support positions are female-dominated I knew that there was about a ninety percent chance of me needing to hire a female. My preference wasn't completely without merit – in my personal life I had very few female friends. I grew up with a father who raced cars and my comfort with males was solidified early on. Men are very no-nonsense, and they tell it like it is. Women are dramatic, catty, and full of passive aggression. When I saw a handful of male applicants come over my desk, I was surprised. Two of them even had the qualifications to warrant an interview. While mulling over applicants, I looked purely at the position laid out for them, and compared it to their experience. At the end of it all, I didn't care if my office assistant was male or female; I just wanted to be sure that I could get along with them.

Of the eighty resumes I received, I called approximately ten in for interviews. I was allowed to do the brunt of the questioning and Randy came in toward the end of each. Randy's addition to each interview was simple, and his line of questioning was delivered in his typical antisocial style.

"Where do you see yourself in five years?"

"How long do you see yourself with the company?"

"What are your salary expectations?"

He would ask his series of questions and leave the room without another word, going back downstairs. The questions had nothing to do with the applicant individually, and were always delivered in the same flat, monotone voice he used when the subject didn't matter to him. He could not have cared less about these interviews. All that he looked forward to at the end of each one was being able to go back downstairs.

All in all, the decision would be mine. In the ad itself, I wrote that I wanted a college student who was looking for a position with a flexible schedule. While I was in college several years earlier, I had trouble finding an employer with the flexibility that I needed. I wanted someone who was working toward a degree, and wanted to help them the way that a former employer had helped me. Some of these applicants hadn't read that part. I had people with food-service backgrounds, retirees, even a couple of high school students. The fact that I had put very specifically what I was looking for and gotten the total opposite made me question my own technique in writing the ad. My first interview was a woman in her mid-forties who spent our entire fifteen minutes begging me to hire her. I understood her need for a position given the state of the job market, but could not make a pity hire just because I felt bad for her. With this as a launching point, I could not see the rest of the interviews going well. There were several people who I thought might work, but whose schedules would not have meshed well with my needs. One of the male applicants had no experience whatsoever, and I could not feel good about hiring someone who I would have to train completely. The other male applicant was a former intern for the Milwaukee Brewers, and Randy wanted me to hire him based on the fact that he was cute. He also wanted to start him at thirteen dollars hourly and have him take on some marketing responsibilities. Since this wasn't something I was looking for, I disregarded Randy's input and just let the interviews continue on. We needed to hire someone who would take on some of my responsibility, not someone to handle marketing.

The one thing that fascinated me about the entire process was how diverse the applicants were. Some seemed to be fed from silver spoons, and others were just making it work the best that they could. I preferred the latter, because I could understand it much better than the former. After my eighth interview, I was really starting to doubt that I would find anyone, until I met Natalie.

Natalie was a twenty-year-old student majoring in poetry, who showed off a visible tattoo when she came into the first interview. She had experience in small offices, and even with payroll and some human resources duties. These were the most important things to me, and when she rattled off what she knew, I couldn't help but smile. She sat and spoke with me for well over twenty minutes during her first interview, and we seemed to get along very well. When Randy met her, he hadn't felt anything for her one way or another, but told me I would be able to make whatever choices I deemed fit.

After my interviews were complete, Randy called me to see what my thoughts were. He gave me his ideas on the people he'd met, but told me that it was still ultimately up to me. My choice was Natalie, and the only discussion we needed to have was how much to pay her. Randy wanted to pay eight dollars hourly, but I talked him up to nine based on her experience and what I believed she could bring to the table. I called Natalie to offer the position to her late on Ralph's last day to start on February 1st, and that phone call eased a bit of the pressure I was dealing with. She accepted, and I told her what to bring with her and what time to arrive the following Monday.

There wasn't any fanfare on Ralph's last day. I toyed around with the idea of buying a card but decided not to at the last minute. For anyone else, there would have been a card, or even a lunch, but not for Ralph. It was a surprise that Randy hadn't wanted to have a party given how much he had grown to hate Ralph over the past six months. I was left with a helpless feeling, knowing what was coming and what I had to look forward to. There were so many questions swirling through my head I felt like a character on the Sims video game with a question mark over my head instead of a green diamond.

Before lunch, Ralph asked me if I could grab some plastic bags when I went home for my lunch break. I did so, and gave them to him as soon as I returned. He used them to pack up his old radio, plants, and other personal things and set them next to his office door, as he got ready to leave. I had spent almost the entire day with Ralph, and was feeling good about the change. I was not completely confident in the way that I should have been, however. As Ralph got ready to leave, I thanked him for showing me everything he had and asked if there were any other little tricks I needed to know. He just told me that he hoped that I found something else soon, and that I would be able to follow in his footsteps. He started to head to the elevator, and I gave him a hug goodbye.

At that moment, Randy decided to call another meeting. He came up the elevator as Ralph was going down the hallway to leave, and they left him no choice but to go back into his office for the proposed 'short' meeting. Randy and Shane called me into Ralph's office, and I sat across from Ralph as Randy shot out a line of questioning, after patronizing us into both explaining what I'd learned that day.

"What did you go over today?"

"We reviewed everything from logging into the stores to entering things into QuickBooks and how to do invoices and cut checks."

"Do you think Liz is ready to take over?"

"No, but I don't think there's any other choice. You want me gone."

"You will be available by phone if she has questions?"

"Yes."

The way that Randy spoke to Ralph during that meeting sickened me. He patronized him, constantly made him repeat himself, and solidified what Ralph had always said about him all along: that he didn't care about anybody but himself. Ralph warned me that I could expect my relationship with Randy to change significantly, only because Randy 'always hates the accountant, because they can never tell him that the business is doing well'. I didn't know if I was more stressed out about becoming an accountant with almost no training, or about how I would be treated by Randy from now on. Ralph's confidence in his interactions with Randy was inspiring. I knew that I would never get away with talking to him the way that Ralph did, but entertaining the thought of standing up for myself was wonderful.

Throughout the meeting, I noticed that Shane was leaning over in his chair, and even putting his hand down toward Ralph's bags, which were set down by the door. At one point, I noticed him very obviously looking into the bags, as if he were attempting to see if Ralph was stealing something. It left me rolling my eyes and putting my attention back to the meeting at hand. At the end of the meeting, Ralph stood up, grabbed his bags, handed his keys to Randy, and left. For all of the bad Friday incidents I had had in the last nine months, this one took the cake. After Ralph was gone, Randy wanted to speak to just me.

"You know that if you have any questions, you can just call Shane right? He has an accounting degree, and he could probably help you with QuickBooks."

While I appreciated the offer, there was no way for me to up and forget that Randy had just told me to get advice from a man who had embezzled thousands from the company. I offered a polite 'thank you'; astounded that Randy would suggest something so absurd.

I had no idea what I was going to do. As I drove home, I just thought 'oh shit' to myself. There was nothing that I *could* do, because Randy had made his decision and I needed to stick to it, no matter how much I didn't want to. I was not at all qualified to be the accountant for this company. There was nothing in my resume that said that I would be, and I had been a near complete failure in any mathematics class I had ever been a part of. I was nervous. There was no way for me to give a hundred percent at both jobs as well as training Natalie in her new position. There are only so many hours in the day, and it was hard for me to continue to let this job monopolize my life. It had done a hell of a job of doing so the past nine months, but I was determined to live a life outside of this office: it could no longer be everything.

FEBRUARY 2009

February, for me, was not a month worth looking forward to. Sure, there was the Hallmark Valentine's Day holiday, but as a single woman I could not have cared less. This would be my first week of doing both accounting and managing the office, but also my first week to spend training Natalie. I was given Ralph's larger office and Natalie was primarily expected to work out of my old one. In a whirlwind of pressure surrounding the completion of financial reports I had no idea about, I spent as much time as possible with Natalie. Using her school schedule as a guide, we crafted her a twenty-five hour workweek, allowing her enough time on either end of the day to catch the necessary public transit to get to school. It was a bit hokey since she would come in mid-morning and leave mid-afternoon most days, but it worked for my needs and it worked for her schedule, which was ostensibly what I wanted.

My dread for training Natalie turned out to be unwarranted, since she was very good at picking up what I asked her to do without having to be shown twice. She picked up the bank deposit verification and answering the phone effortlessly, and I added new responsibilities daily, which she was comfortable with. By the end of her first week, Natalie was handling a good half of my former duties, including payroll entry and dealing with our new hires. This lifted a significant amount of pressure from my shoulders.

My new responsibilities, on the other hand, were one headache after another. All that I had was the step-by-step list of duties I'd written down in the form of five pages of typed notes. I was comfortable with about seventy percent of what I was doing, but the other thirty percent left something to be desired. Ralph had dreamt up no fewer than ten spreadsheet reports to send to Randy on a weekly basis, and had only shown me how to do half of them. The half he showed me had been the "easy half", and included an outstanding check report, and spreadsheets exported from QuickBooks reports. The exported reports included both accounts payable and receivable summaries, as well as a detailed list of unpaid bills. The reports I had not been shown were of course the more difficult ones, which included a food cost report and credit card deposit report. The food cost report had never been explained to me, and the credit card report was relatively easy to figure out. All it took was adding up the various deposits made to our credit card account daily, and multiplying the total by a percentage. I attempted to figure out the food cost report several times and even e-mailed Randy for help, but never received a reply. Apparently, the report had not meant much.

The first job I decided on as it related to the accounting was reorganizing Ralph's former office. There was no rhyme or reason to his recordkeeping whatsoever, and his idea of filing was piles of labeled folders. The files on his computer were difficult to sift through, and took two days alone to reorganize. The paper files took the rest of the week and with Natalie's help, I was able to get it all done. Working was much easier now that I could navigate my office, and I was growing more and more confident as the days passed. Cutting checks, data entry, even those weekly reports all got easier. I had a clearer head in my new office than I ever had in my old one, and found myself getting excited about my first couple of weeks as a glorified number cruncher. It amazed me that a week's worth of organization had made me so excited about accounting – in a way it was easier than office management. The biggest reason was because there were much fewer interactions with others and fewer interruptions, but it only served as the calm before the storm.

Late in the second weekend of the month, I made a Sunday afternoon trip to the Ikea store in Schaumburg, Illinois. I had never been before, and was perhaps a little too excited about the photo frames and household storage items I purchased. At 9:00 PM, I received a phone call from Randy. As was customary, I let the call go to voicemail. When I listened to the voicemail, I found out that Randy was intending to rearrange the office, and wanted me to come down to the building to help. I returned his call immediately, telling him that on any other night I would have, but I was tired from the trip to Illinois I had taken that day. He said okay, and I told him that I had worked hard to reorganize my new office, and that if he could make the minimum number of changes there, I would appreciate it. He told me that he would try, and that he would see me in the morning. Naively, I thought that he might stick to his word, but I was shown just how stupid that was when I walked into the office the next morning.

Everything in the waiting area had either disappeared or been moved, and the leather couch was nowhere to be found. Instead of the couch, there was a glass-topped desk from The Sharper Image, and our impressive view of downtown Milwaukee had been covered up by a four-drawer filing cabinet and our rack of paperwork for new hires and current employees. I noticed that Ralph's former PC was situated under the new desk, and the computer monitor from my old office had been set up on top. What I took from this was I was expected to sit in the main room of the office, since Ralph's old computer had become mine. This made no sense to me, as I was to be dealing with all of the confidential company financials. Upset, I journeyed down to the hall to the office Natalie had previously been occupying to find the gigantic monitor that had been in Ralph's office set on top of the laptop and dock I had been using for the past two months. My framed pictures had all been moved back into my old office, and at that point I was both angry and confused. So far, my things were spread between two offices, and I found the rest stacked in a box in Ralph's old office, which was now empty. Grabbing the box and checking the desk itself for anything they may have missed, I brought it up to what I envisioned was my new "office", setting out to get myself reorganized. I attempted to call Randy once I had calmed down about a half hour after arriving. As usual, he didn't answer and didn't call back. Natalie came in just as stumped as I was, and I was in no mood to talk so just sent her into my old office to work for the day. I don't know that I was angry about the change itself, but I know that I was upset that my things had been moved without even a short note to explain things. I finally got my call back from Randy at about 4 PM, asking me to come to the weekly manager's meeting and drop off a set of menu box topper photocopies for the stores. This particular day, I was supposed to be leaving early to pick my roommate, Sam, up from the dentist, because he had his wisdom teeth removed earlier in the day. Regretfully, I agreed, and said I would be there as soon as I could.

With it impossible to hide my upset once I arrived at the meeting, I put on a happy face and attempted to hide my disgust with the new office overhaul. Of course, Randy knew that I would be upset, and called me into his office for an impromptu meeting that I waited almost 45 minutes for. On any other day, it would not have bothered me, but on this particular day I needed to pick up my roommate's prescription and could not wait around. Sitting in Randy's office, I was visibly uncomfortable and he picked up on it immediately.

"What's the matter with you today?"

"I was upset all day because of the office, and I really need to go and get Sam's prescription."

"What's wrong with the office?"

"You moved all of my stuff to three different places, Randy. I had no idea where to start."

"Shane, Tim and I were moving the office until 3 AM. I thought you would be happy and would be thanking me."

"Why would I be happy when it makes my job that much harder? I asked you to leave my office alone, because I spent all last week organizing it."

"So now you get to organize it again. Liz, I don't think that you have any reason to be angry."

"How would you feel if someone went into your office and completely reorganized everything without your input?"

"Liz, I called and asked you if you wanted a part in it. You said no."

"It was 9 PM when you called me, and I was exhausted."

"That's not my problem."

"Why didn't you just leave my office alone like I asked?"

"Shane needed an office, and I decided to give him Ralph's old one."

"So you moved me out to the lobby so Shane could have an office?"

"Why were you in the lobby? Liz, you're supposed to be in your old office."

"I didn't know! I tried to call you and you didn't pick up. You could have somehow let me know what I was walking into."

"Liz, I feel like you're ungrateful for what I've done for you. I gave you health insurance after thirty days instead of ninety, and have increased your income over twenty percent. You have no right to be upset about how I chose to reorganize the office."

At that point in the conversation, I was speechless. There was nothing that I could do to change Randy's mind, and if I kept fighting I would be there all night. I knew better than to try and fight back.

I had no idea what anything in the past had to do with the office being moved around. He had given me insurance early, after I explained how much my medications cost. He had increased my pay, and for that I was thankful. I never thought that he would hold those things against me, but I was wrong. I left without resolution on either side of things but instead a promise for a meeting the next morning. While I was in my car on the way to the pharmacy, I realized that I was angrier than before I had arrived, although I didn't know how. I couldn't even fathom the conversation that had just taken place, and that night was the beginning of the end of any residual warm-and-fuzzies I got from my job.

The next day, I reorganized my things once again, this time in my old office. I hoped that the third time would be the charm, and that this would be the last time. The space was much smaller than in Ralph's office, and it was difficult to fit the files and other items I needed on my desk. My original office was about half the size of Ralph's former one, and was an odd shape whereas Ralph's was squarer. There were filing cabinets lining nearly all of the wall space within, and there was barely space for my oversized desk in the center. Add the computer dock, oversized monitor, lamp, phone, and desk calculator into the mix, and there was no space for the files I needed to have at my fingertips, much less open desk space. Though I was upset, I still tried to make the best of the bad situation I was given. I crammed everything I could onto the surface of the desk, everything in my accounts payable and receivable expanding files finding a new home on the floor. While many people may have just accepted the change, I could not bring myself to do it.

From day one, Randy had constantly been telling me to take ownership of not only my job, but also my space. This was the first time I had done so, spare putting up some framed photos of friends and family, and it had gotten me nowhere. I spent a week taking ownership over my new office, and it was all destroyed within the course of a six-hour power trip. How could he expect me to work efficiently when I was left wondering what else would be different every day when I arrived? Every day I was taken down one more notch – I was constantly questioned on the bank balances and how I completed my assignments. At one point, Randy requested to sit in with me while I entered bills and did simple data entry, which of course never happened. Every day, I felt what little ownership I had in my position dwindling further and further. I didn't know whether my age played a part, but could not help but think that it was a big reason for my constant micromanaging. I could not see his lines of questioning and flat-out screwing with me happening if I was ten or twenty years older.

Shortly before Ralph's departure, we had had a conversation that stuck in my head while I thought all of this through. During one of my final days in training with him, the subject of my employment came up. In this conversation he candidly discussed my multiple interviews, and stated that there were people much better qualified to do the job than I was. I understood this – I had applied to the job not thinking that I had a snowball's chance in hell. What had it all come down to? My age. Randy hired me knowing that I was inexperienced, but that I would be happy taking much less compensation than the others in the running. I found out soon after my employment began that I had been Randy's third choice, at least. This was discovered while I was reorganizing Helen's computer files during my first week and found an offer letter for someone else. I knew that I applied for the job not thinking I would get an interview, much less the job itself. What started out as a stroke of luck had become a nightmare.

After the office's reorganization, I cut all ties with Randy outside of work hours. I didn't answer text messages or phone calls, and limited my conversations with him significantly. If he could not honor one simple request, how could I trust him with anything else? Randy got the point. As days turned into weeks, the texts and calls dwindled before stopping completely.

One Wednesday evening, they started again. I had returned home for the day and was in the shower, hearing my text message tone about eight times in two minutes. Knowing that I would never receive that many in such a short time from a sane person, I knew that it had to be Randy. Once I was finished, I checked my phone and found that my suspicions had been true – eight text messages from Randy.

R: Liz, I need you to send me your voicemail password.
R: Liz, I need that password.
R: Still waiting…
R: …
R: Liz, I need you to send me that password immediately.
R: …
R: Why aren't you answering my texts?
R: I need that password.

I was absolutely stunned. First, at the sheer volume of text messages, and then at the annoyance that was obvious as I read further down my iPhone's touch screen. It was almost 9 PM, what would be so pressing that he would need to check my voicemail?

L: Why do you need my voicemail password? I was in the shower.

R: I need it for my password file.

L: I didn't know you kept one.

R: Please give me your voicemail password.

Randy was about as slick as butter getting me to give up that password. I knew for a fact that he didn't have a password file, and that he had only wanted it so that his micromanaging could escalate even further. Not wanting the situation to get worse, I gave him the password.

The next morning, I had an e-mail asking questions about all of the phone messages that had come in that night. When I went to check the messages so I could reply, they had all been deleted. How could I answer questions about messages that I had never listened to? I replied by simply saying I could not answer questions about the messages since someone had taken the liberty of deleting them. I never received a reply to that e-mail, and changed my voicemail password. Surprisingly, Randy never mentioned anything else about his password file.

In short, I was looking forward to my day off that Friday. I was going back to my hometown of Green Bay on Thursday night to see Motley Crue with a handful of friends, and had a doctor appointment the next morning and a dental appointment that afternoon to get a cavity filled. I was also looking forward to it just to spend time with my family, who I hadn't seen in about a month. After an amazing show and going out to a handful of bars on Thursday night, I headed home and fell asleep. Since this was Natalie's first day in the office without me, I had told her ahead of time that I would be available for her all day if she had questions or needed help with anything. There had been several calls throughout the day, on topics ranging from how to complete the manager payroll to general office duties. I felt that she did fine, and she truly didn't call me unless she needed something important.

Before I left, I had been working with some of our accounts payable items and hadn't put the expanding file away, but had attempted to straighten up my desk. There was nowhere to put it, given the small space, and I did the best I could to make sure that things were cleaned up. At 5:30

PM on the dot, I got another phone call from Natalie. Thinking that it was no big deal, I answered the phone.

"Randy wants to speak to you."

"Ok."

I was put on hold.

"Liz, why wasn't your office cleaned up before you left?"

"I did the best I could to clean up so that I would not forget what I was doing on Monday morning."

"Liz, your office is filthy. This is completely unacceptable."

"Randy, I did the best that I could to clean up before I left. I lost track of time last night and needed to leave."

"You should have taken fifteen minutes to clean up after yourself."

"I had already been there fifteen minutes late. I had to leave. I'm sorry."

"I may never let you take another long weekend. This is unacceptable."

"I'm sorry. I don't know what else you want me to say."

"I don't want to have this happen again."

And then he hung up on me.

No sooner had the call ended than I had two new e-mail notifications on my phone. Randy had sent not one, but two separate messages expressing his upset over what he called my "filthy" office. One was a play-by-play of everything he'd said to me in the phone call, and the other went further and explained why he was upset and exactly why he had been disappointed. In reality, it wasn't a big deal. To any other boss, it would not have mattered one way or another; it would not make a difference to them either way. Since I worked for the boss sent straight from hell, there was no way to rationalize whatsoever. I came to grips with that months before, and it had only taken this long for it to manifest itself into my daily work life.

MARCH 2009

I had been asking about how to do the weekly food cost report since early February, and it wasn't until a few days into March that I got any semblance of an answer. There was e-mail from Randy from the previous Friday asking about the food cost report and why it had not been completed. I replied to tell him that I didn't know where the information was supposed to come from, and that I had asked him for it several times. I even went so far as to forward him the e-mails to prove that I wasn't making anything up. Shortly after, I received a short e-mail giving me backwards answers as to how the report needed to be completed. The information would come from several sources: the franchise's web-based store summary program, weekly food invoices, and weekly operating and inventory reports from the stores themselves. After he gave me this information, Randy seemed to think that I would immediately be able to do over a month's worth of reports. He both e-mailed and called me several times within the next two hours, expecting them to be finished. I told him that I would try as hard as I could to get them done by the end of the day, and I thought that would be the end of it.

Several hours later, I received a phone call from Shane wanting to know why the food cost report wasn't done. Didn't these guys talk to each other? They were attached at the hip, but one didn't seem to know which way was up without the other. I told Shane the same thing that I had told Randy – that I was teaching myself how to do this report, and that once it was ready I would send it over. This didn't stop Shane from coming upstairs and standing in the corner of my office ten minutes later to supervise my progress for at least fifteen. After fifteen minutes elapsed, I turned to him and asked if he could find something else to do in the most polite way I possibly could. It seemed like he didn't understand why I would be asking that – because normal people can do their jobs with some jerk with his arms crossed in their peripheral vision. Eventually, he left, and the reports got finished by the end of the day, just as I'd promised.

There was something amiss with Randy and Shane lately, and it was hard for me to tell exactly what it was. I had caught Shane coming in on the lobby camera several days that week, which was strange. Typically, he parked his car in the second floor parking garage, and I never knew when he came or went. The rumors flying around the company still said that Shane stayed over at Randy's on a regular basis, which would not be difficult to prove, given that he never seemed to leave. It would be a fluke to see Randy without Shane either at his side or following closely, and when these things weren't happening, I knew something had to be going on.

Following the voicemail password incident, I hadn't received any phone calls or text messages from Randy outside of work hours. When I got a phone call at 9:30 PM the day after the food cost report issue, I was surprised. Part of me said to let it go to voicemail, but the other part of me wondered why he would be calling me so late, especially given the rocky nature of our relationship. After the third ring, I decided to answer.

"Liz, do you think I can make this company work without Shane?"

This was a conversation we had on several occasions, after I told Randy that as much as he cared about Shane, that Shane didn't do his job. He routinely missed doing simple paperwork, never got information in on time, and everyone else's work suffered because of it. Shane and I weren't friends, and hadn't been for a long time. To me, he was like the self-obsessed, moronic older brother who thought he knew everything there was, but could not find his way out of a paper bag without help.

"I've told you how I feel about that before. You know that you could make it work. You made it work before, and you could make it work again. There is nothing stating that Shane has to have anything to do with this company. I know that you don't want to get rid of him, but I think that things will only get worse if he stays."

"I don't have to get rid of him."

"Why not?"

"Shane quit."

When Randy told me this, my brain was going a mile a minute. I wanted to know what happened, but the rational side of me was saying that the less I knew, the better. He had obviously called me for advice, and I did the best I could to give it to him, though I didn't want to get too involved. The rest of the conversation centered on Randy explaining what had happened, whether I wanted to know or not.

They had been arguing for days, and there had been rumors of an explosion between the two of them happening inside one of our stores.

Randy could be incredibly demanding, and Shane had started to crack under the pressure of constant micromanagement and being forced to stay near Randy at all times. Because he had stolen money in the past, Randy kept him close as if to make sure it didn't happen again. Randy had been monopolizing Shane's life for at least the last six months, and I was personally surprised that he had not left sooner. Earlier in the phone conversation, Randy said that Shane even took out his garbage for him. Shane had walked out of Randy's apartment after having another row, and in the heat of a verbal altercation had told Randy that he would regret everything, and that he would do what he could to take the company down. What this meant, I didn't know. I wanted to think that it was nothing more than Shane making empty threats, which wasn't completely uncommon. Randy called to ask for my advice, and I found myself repeating what I always said.

"You know that you can do this without him. You did it before you found him, and you can do it now that he's gone."

Randy was upset about Shane storming out, but seemed optimistic about what I was telling him. He asked me to have the elevator codes for both the office and his personal apartment changed in the morning (Shane had codes for both), and stated that he would be changing many of the computer passwords as well. When I hung up the phone after a nearly two-hour conversation, I felt a tiny bit of optimism after immediately pulling a swig out of my emergency bottle of Jagermeister. In the back of my mind however, I knew that Shane wasn't gone for long.

Surprise didn't even begin to cover my feeling when I went through the entire next day without seeing or hearing from Shane. My optimism had grown, thinking that this would be the actual breaking point for the two of them – maybe Shane really was gone for good.

Midway through the afternoon, Randy called me to see if I would come out to the airport to return a rental car with him, and give him a ride back to the building. I felt a little bad for him, so I agreed to do so. He told me that it would be "in a little while", but we didn't leave the office until almost 5:30 PM, when I was supposed to be done at 6 PM. I figured that we might avoid traffic, so I would still be done at my usual time. Randy got onto the freeway first, in the white rental Jeep. I followed behind him, and didn't find out until halfway through the trip that he had absolutely no idea where he was going. I texted him simple directions, and he had stayed in a lane that made it impossible for him to move over in time for the exit. We wound up turning around at a nearby exit to switch places, because I had driven to the airport previously and actually knew where I was going. After arriving, Randy had to bring the Jeep back into the rental company's parking garage. I drove into the garage behind him, but there was nowhere for me to park. I wound up in a traffic lane with my four-way flashers on while I waited. He had to go into the terminal to return the car, and I sat in my car for nearly a half hour waiting for him. By this time, it was almost 6:30, and I was antsy to be done for the day. When he came back, he said that we still needed to unload the Jeep, and I wound up ducking under a fence within the garage in order to assist him. There were envelopes, box topper menus, and towels, which were a good two armloads worth. Of course, Randy could not carry a thing, and I wound up staggering back to my car with a full armload of paper and dirty towels. Tossing them into my trunk unceremoniously, I was ready to get him dropped off and get on with my night.

"Do you think we could stop at the Capitol store on the way back?"

The Capitol store was nowhere near on the way back from the airport to the apartment building. As much as I wanted to say no and assert to him that I needed to get home, I still felt badly for him and agreed. I had known from the moment he asked me to help him with the rental car that he was going to want to go somewhere else.

Randy constantly made Shane chauffer him around, even in his own car. If he didn't have to, Randy never drove anywhere. He had done this to me on a few other occasions, and I hated it. I figured if I said no that he would be upset, and I didn't want to have to deal with him in that state again. He was still my boss, after all.

As soon as I walked into the store with Randy, the ribbing began. Thankfully, two of my favorite managers were working – one the general manager, and the other the assistant. Laughing when she saw what was going on, the assistant manager asked me if I "was the new Shane", and asked how it felt to run a limo service. Before we walked in, I noticed a pile of broken glass and a dead rat near the entry door. When I got the general manager alone for a few minutes (or so I thought), I told him the things were out there and that customers could see them when they came in. He told me that he knew, but that he hadn't had any time to take care of it, and really didn't want to.

Surprisingly, Randy only took about twenty minutes at the store. Upon leaving, however, I was barraged with comments I hadn't been expecting.

"Liz, you aren't the boss of the managers. You have no right to tell them what to do."

"What are you talking about?"

"The rat and the glass."

"I didn't think I was out of line, I was just telling him they were there."

"It's inappropriate and you don't need to do it."

"OK. I didn't think it was inappropriate. I told him that he could give me a plastic bag and I would clean it up myself, but you wanted to leave."

That was as far as it went. It seemed that Randy liked telling people what to do, but didn't like when they rationalized with him. There had been more conversations between the two of us dropped due to that reason than I could count on two hands. After the store incident, I made a beeline back to the apartment building. I didn't have a problem spending the extra time with Randy (unpaid, of course), but it was now almost 8 PM, and I began receiving text messages and phone calls asking when I would be home. Randy attempted to get me to come upstairs and 'hang out' when we got back, but I just shook my head and feigned exhaustion, stating that I needed to go home and go to bed. He was disappointed, but I wasn't about to fall back into the habit of phone calls and text messages. I had learned all too well the last time it had happened. As soon as I dropped Randy off, I finally felt free. I could not believe that a simple trip to the airport had turned into a nearly three-hour long debacle, and realized I actually was exhausted from the time spent with Randy.

The next afternoon, I half expected Randy to want me to drive him somewhere. Imagine my surprise when Shane came up the elevator, without a word about his disappearance the day before as if nothing had happened two days earlier. In a way, I was angry – Randy had wasted my time to give him advice he would never use – but at the same time, I was crushed. If Shane was back, there was no way that the company could improve. There was no chance, and I was disgusted and disappointed in myself for thinking that Randy could actually have willpower in relation to Shane and his own feelings.

Several days later, I found out the story behind Shane's return. Randy hadn't wanted to be home yet when I dropped him off, and called Shane to see if they could 'talk through their issues'. Shane stayed at the building until almost 4 AM, and they had 'just talked'. Beyond that conversation, I did not want to know a thing about what went on between he and Shane behind closed doors. I was going right back to not talking to either Randy or Shane outside of work hours unless absolutely necessary, and felt my constant proverbial headache lifting.

The disgust I felt for the entire situation surrounding my boss and his 'golden boy' was incredibly obvious to Randy. I attempted to make nice with Shane for Randy's sake, but didn't go out of my way to make him happy either way. He was still not getting me information I directly requested from him, and he was still just as useless as before he left. I wondered what the two of them did all day, but squashed that thought as soon as it came through my brain because really, I didn't want to know.

The week after Shane's quitting drama, a general manager by the name of Mitch came in to pick up some box topper menus and some deposit slips. He had also come in to ask me what I thought about a marketing idea he had. We were spending a lot of money on direct mail marketing, but constantly got offers for free marketing and advertising from vendors and non-profits. Mitch had received one and wanted to take advantage of it, and wanted to know just how effective I thought they would be. I designed some flyers for Mitch in the past, and he was asking me if I would be okay with doing another one if the deal went through. After spending all day every day since the beginning of February buried in accounting, it was nice to help with something creative, even if we only wound up talking about it for twenty minutes. When Randy got the gist of me talking about marketing and not accounting, he called Mitch into the back conference room and told him (in more words) to leave me alone. He also sent me a text message:

R: Liz, I need you focused on accounting. If the managers want to speak to someone about marketing, they can speak to Shane or myself.

That had been downright rude on Randy's part. I was not doing anything to purposefully upset him by talking about marketing; I was just letting Mitch bounce ideas off of me, because he had done it in the past. After Randy sent the text message, he called me into the conference room and went on another tangent about how he needed me focused on accounting and nothing but. I explained to him that I had helped Mitch with marketing materials before, and that had been the only reason he'd approached me. Ignoring everything that came out of my mouth, Randy continued to repeat the same three words: focused on accounting. I had been eating, sleeping, and breathing accounting since January. I didn't think it was too much to ask to let me have twenty minutes of a single day to talk about something else. Randy didn't echo this feeling, and could not fathom why I would ever avoid accounting in favor of something more creative. Any sane person would do the same thing.

Being micromanaged day in and day out had gotten old weeks before. I had two different people giving me different things to do at different times, and it was difficult for me to keep everything straight. Shane stated that he would deal with the separate phone bill for one of our suburban store locations, and I took him at his word and assumed that I would not need to cut a check for it. The day immediately following the marketing issue, Randy came in to see me, telling me that the store's phones had been shut off.

"Liz, the phones at Kenosha were turned off."

"Shane took the bill from me weeks ago, and told me he would deal with it."

"Why would he do that?"

"I don't know. That was what he implied to me, and I was under the impression that he was taking care of it."

"Liz, I don't believe that he would do that."

"He took the bill. I don't even have it anymore."

"How can we take care of this?"

"You are going to have to call the phone company and arrange payments."

"Can you do it?"

"I don't have the bill."

"I will get in touch with Shane and see that it is taken care of."

Dead air. Any time that I brought up Shane not doing his job directly to Randy, he completely closed himself off. Whether it was hanging up phone calls without a word or not talking to me unless he could not avoid it, it was completely obvious to me that he didn't believe me. Though I had tangible proof, he still would not believe that Shane was doing as awfully as he was. Miraculously, the phones were back on approximately a half hour after my phone call with Randy, and nothing was mentioned about it after the fact. From that point forward, however, checks were always cut promptly and Shane took no bills, at least not to my knowledge.

The old adage "the calm before the storm" once again came into play here. It was exactly one week to the day after the phone disconnection, and Randy came into my office. Things had been stagnant; not many issues, and I had been left alone to work for the most part. When Randy came into my office that morning, however, I knew that something had to be going on. He rarely spoke to me unless he absolutely had to, and I was surprised that he would meet with me without Shane's supervision. He had been quiet – almost too quiet – and I was not ready for the bomb he was about to drop on me.

"Liz, I want to let you know about what direction I'm planning to take the company in. There are going to be some pretty big changes, and I don't want you to have any questions."

"What kinds of changes?"

"I am bringing the company into bankruptcy. This will not affect you or your job, but will wipe out all of our debt and we will be able to get a clean slate."

"How long will it take? When will you file?"

"It should take a couple of months to get everything together, and I will let you know when I file. I don't want this information to leave this office. Do you have any questions for me?"

How could I have questions? I was too busy being absolutely stunned to even form a coherent sentence. After coming out to me months before, I always dreaded when he would come into my office and close the door. One thing stuck out to me, though – momentarily, I still held onto my fear that he was coming in to tell me what an awful job I was doing and wanting to find someone else. While the subject hadn't been that, it was quite a bomb to drop on me.

While I had very little accounting experience, I had even less experience with bringing a business into bankruptcy. After Randy's departure from my office, I did everything that I could to not only look up the different types of bankruptcy for a business, but how long it took to file and what it meant. Randy said that he was not putting the company into flat-out bankruptcy, but into a re-organization. This meant that all of our old debt would disappear, and that we would be able to start out fresh. I knew that if this bankruptcy actually did go through that the slate wouldn't remain clean for long, but kept that observation to myself.

A mere three days after telling me that the company's bankruptcy would not affect me, Randy called me late in the afternoon on Friday to tell me that I would need to get a new phone, as he could "no longer carry my phone on his plan due to the bankruptcy". This was his personal mobile phone plan, which had nothing to do with the business, and I had $25 removed from my paychecks each week in order to pay my portion of each monthly bill. There was no reason for him to do this to me besides just being Randy. I was told that I had the weekend to get a new phone, and that my iPhone service would be cancelled the following Monday.

This would be no easy feat for me, because of my questionable credit rating. It was difficult for me to start new phone contracts, and I did not really want to. Stressed out, I went home and talked to my roommate, Sam, about it, and he agreed to add a line to his phone plan. He would extend his single plan to a family plan, and we would split the bill halfway. We were planning to look at new apartments that Saturday, and just went to the phone store beforehand to handle everything. While I didn't know what to do with my old phone as of yet, I was busy texting my friends and calling family to give them my new phone number when not one, but two phone calls from Shane came in on my iPhone.

The first call was asking me for my computer password. Why this was constantly an issue for Randy and Shane I never knew. I could hear Randy in the background of the phone call, and Shane was repeating everything I overheard him saying. Not wanting to argue because it was Saturday and I wasn't supposed to be on call, I just gave him the password and didn't bother playing games.

Twenty minutes later, I received another call from Shane. This time, he questioned me about a letter I wrote for a former employee in June 2008. This letter stated the employee's first and last dates of employment, and their pay rate and reason for leaving. It was not a very involved letter, and definitely not one that I saw myself being questioned for nine months later. The letter had been so that the employee could get food stamps, and there was never a question of needing prior approval before writing it or sending it out. Shane scolded me and told me that it could not happen again. While thinking about it, I realized once again that Shane wasn't my boss, but since Randy was his puppeteer I took it as if Randy had told me himself. Going back once more, this also reminded me of months earlier when I had been scolded for giving Dylan, a former general manager his pay stubs. What I could do nine months after the fact was lost on me, but I agreed to whatever he said in the interest of getting him off of the phone. He also informed me that Randy wanted me to return my iPhone on Monday – something I viewed as a gift. I wondered if Randy would start asking for my other gifts back too, such as my small birthday and Christmas gifts. Concentrating on having a good day and not wanting to worry myself, I turned off my iPhone for one of the last times, and disconnected myself for the remainder of the weekend. During this time, I went through different feelings; those of disgust and anger, and I realized that if I really and truly cut all ties outside of work hours, that I would not have to worry about it anymore. Throughout the weekend, I solidified this decision by questioning friends and family, who asked why I hadn't come to the decision sooner.

Monday morning, I brought my iPhone back as I was asked to. I brought the original package and all of its' accessories and paperwork. Nothing was said, though Randy came and picked it up. When he came to pick up his payroll and supplies for the weekly manager's meeting, I asked to speak to him.

"What can I help you with?"

"Randy, I don't want to do this, but I don't want to be contacted on the weekends or outside of work anymore, unless it is an emergency."

"Can I ask why this is? Why is this something I was never alerted to before?"

"Over the weekend, I was called twice by Shane, and there have been countless evenings and days when you yourself have sent me text messages or asked me to 'hang out'. I am interested in having a professional relationship, but outside of that I am asking to be left alone."

"Liz, you realize that if you do this that things will change."

"What will change? It means nothing about my willingness or ability to complete my job. I am respectfully asking that the calls and texts outside of work stop."

"You are doing this over two phone calls?"

"No, Randy. I am doing this because I never know whether or not I can live my personal life since there is no way to know when I am going to get a phone call or text message."

"I was under the impression that you didn't have a problem with it."

"Now that I'm no longer using the iPhone that you got for me, I should not be required to be available 24 hours a day. I am an hourly employee, and I want to be treated as such."

"Things are going to change, I hope you realize that. But I will honor your request."

Following that, there was complete radio silence. Not only that, but in the days after the meeting itself, Randy barely spoke to me. He would not answer calls that I made to him from the office, and would only speak to me through calling and asking Natalie to relay messages to me. When he came up to the office in the elevator, he would not even acknowledge my presence. Truly, since I was no longer using the phone he had purchased for me, I should not have been obligated to be available 24 hours a day. As I told him, I was an hourly employee and not salaried, and any sane person would have asked the contact to stop just as soon as it started. I took responsibility for letting it happen for such a long time, but in some ways, I felt as if I had sold my soul and given away my personal life for the luxury of having an iPhone. At that point, none of that mattered anymore and all I wanted was the ability to breathe a sigh of relief. While I was convinced that already, Randy's treatment was reminiscent of the way he'd treated Ralph, I tried not to think too much into it and considered the source. As he had told me initially, my position was "a lifestyle, not a job", and after almost a year, I was unconvinced that it was the lifestyle I wanted.

For the duration of my employment, getting most office supplies was part of my job. The first two months of my employment, I had a petty cash account. I used petty cash for these supplies, but Randy discontinued it without reason and the supplies were now my financial responsibility. I was typically given an expense check after much headache and many requests. In my entire employment, I had only ever put monies spent on supplies on my expense check, and attempted to ignore the hundreds of miles I'd put on my personal vehicle without so much as batting an eyelash. Even when gasoline was almost five dollars per gallon, I never asked to have my mileage reimbursed. The headache would have been much more than it was worth, and I shoved it all to the side in favor of a tolerable work environment.

After nearly a week of the silent treatment, I gave Randy an expense report for $24.90. I had been asked to buy stamps and some other items, and figured that a check for that small amount would not have been a big deal. After waiting several days, I questioned Randy on it, and he told me that he needed to get prior approval to write checks. That day, I had printed many checks for bills that he had no issue signing. My questioning had caused him to print the expense check, but he refused to sign it. Why did everything have to be such a headache? Was there nothing easy in this job anymore? Everything seemed to get more and more petty, and there was no reasoning behind it. Randy was just trying to get under my skin.

APRIL 2009

From the beginning of April onward, it was blatantly obvious that the battle lines had been drawn. This battle wasn't the guns-blazing-six-shooting type, however. It was a silent battle of wits and psychology. From something so small as an expense check (which I received on the first) to day-to-day interaction, it wasn't difficult to see that Randy didn't like me. My interaction with him soon shifted from slim to none, and it seemed as though he got more and more petty as time went on. In early April, the key for the downstairs mailbox was taken away from me, because apparently Randy "had to get the mail as a condition of the bankruptcy". This meant that I got mail once a week, if that. I rarely received replies to e-mails no matter their importance, and while it grated on me, it was all part of what I aptly titled "the game".

When anyone did something that didn't fit into Randy and Shane's plan, their first idea was to get rid of them as quickly and unceremoniously as possible. Whether it was nitpicking what they did during work hours or making something up completely out of the blue, it was almost always successful. The thing about it was that they were terrible at covering themselves, and many of the people who were affected applied for unemployment, and received it. In many cases, the issues were absolutely ridiculous and were no basis on which to fire someone. It seemed that if they wanted you gone, you were gone, but if you did something for them, they would let anything that you did or any rules you broke fall to the wayside. A perfect example of this was Nicki, the store manager that Shane was still sleeping with. She had routinely been reported selling drugs and using marijuana in the store, as well as drinking with her employees. Nothing was ever done, and it was all swept under the rug.

There was no even playing field for any of our employees. Their employment was continued out of convenience from Randy and Shane, but if you did anything to stand up for yourself, they would get rid of you as quickly as possible. I could see that this was turning into the beginning of trying to get rid of me, but they had no reasoning. I came in every day, did what I was asked to do, and had only asked Randy to stop contacting me outside of work hours. This was no reason to be terminated, but I guessed that it was the next step in Randy and Shane's master plan.

The only other aspect of the situation that I had ascertained was that Randy never liked the accountant. Randy was awful at managing his business, and it showed in the haphazard way in which his stores were run and issues with employees handled. He would often call on our vendors to handle problems in our stores, but never wanted to pay the bills, no matter how small. For example, there was an unpaid bill from a plumbing company for less than $200 which had gone to collections, an unpaid bill from a glass company for less than $250 also sent to collections – and the list went on. The accountant's job was to cut checks and handle financial reports, but they were not given the freedom to do so. Whenever a check was needed, it had to be requested from Randy, and if he didn't feel like paying the bill, he wouldn't. As the accountant, I dealt with phone calls from vendors on a constant basis, asking where their money was. I would give them an honest answer, letting them know that I didn't control which bills were paid, but that I had to get checks from Randy before I could pay anything, and had no control over what got paid when. Oftentimes, they understood, but for the small amount that didn't, they would berate me and demand to speak to Randy. I gave out his mobile phone number several times without a second thought, only because I felt awful for these people who did us a service and now weren't being paid because Randy had no clue how to run a business. Other reasons that Randy didn't like the accountant were simple: the accountant could never tell him what he wanted to hear. Thinking that we had a good weekend or a good day and that it would clear up our financial problems, Randy never understood that the problems were much deeper and older than a $20,000 week at a store. While thinking he was the best thing to happen to world of pizza, the people he dealt with and his employees all felt very much the opposite. Randy was nothing but a little boy in a man's body. He would pout and have fits when he didn't get his way. He was alone in life, and had no friends outside of the friends he paid.

One thing that I was never given upon starting my job was a true representation of what I was getting myself into. It took my own experiences for me to figure out that a self-obsessed compulsive psychopath ran this place, and that I was expected to smile, nod, and accept everything that happened. Helen had done it, and now I was expected to do the same. If I had known that I was walking into a living, breathing soap opera, I would have run screaming. It would have made an interesting interview, anyway.

Rethinking these things when it came to Natalie, I decided that I was going to tell her the different things I witnessed throughout the duration of my employment. As she was expected to represent the company, I felt that she deserved to know to what lengths Randy and Shane would go to screw people over, as well as the real way things were run and handled. Since she had been with the company for over two months, I was sure that she had her own ideas. We had a great rapport from day one, and I trusted her with the information I gave her. One afternoon midway through the month, I sat down with Natalie and told her everything. I told her about Shane's theft and affair, as well as the different things I'd seen happen from managers getting screwed out of money weekly to the ridiculous reasons some employees had been fired. If Randy knew I had told her this, he would have blown a gasket, but it put my mind at ease. I felt that I did Natalie a favor by telling her, so that she would not have to go through living and learning the way that I had. Some of the things she could not believe, and many she could see happening, even though she had only been with the company for a short time. Luckily, I documented some of the bigger issues, so I could prove them true easily.

The reason that I informed Natalie of the company history was because I trusted her. I felt that she should be given the full picture of her employer, instead of being slapped with the cold truth of reality when the time came. I knew that she would not tell Randy or Shane anything that I said, and she knew that I did it for her benefit. I didn't do it out of spite, although I could have when thinking about what had happened. The only other reason? I didn't have anything to lose, even if Randy did catch wind. I was confident that he wouldn't.

When looking at the inner workings of the company – Randy, Shane, Natalie and myself – it seemed as if we had been divided into teams in order to play a wicked game of kickball, instead of working together as a cohesive unit to keep the franchise running smoothly. Obviously, there were two teams, and every day was another match: Team Randy and Shane versus Team Liz and Natalie. Their side was insanely irrational, while our side was normal and levelheaded. Sitting in the office all day every day, it was not uncommon to not hear from Randy or to not see him at all. He was typically sitting in his office directly downstairs and felt that calling upstairs to bark orders would be a better way to do business.

The entire franchise was being run by a 21-year-old office assistant and a 23-year-old office manager (and self-taught accountant). Our employer was almost never available by phone unless calling him four or more times, and there was a large sense of disconnection between the two sides. There was no real explanation for the treatment or actions of Randy's 'team', though the office staff seemed to have a finer grasp on the way things were supposed to work than even he did. If another esteemed businessman or franchise owner walked into our office, they would either rip their hair out or insist on Randy getting a lobotomy.

After having my extended conversation with Natalie about my knowledge of the past year, I was surprised to have Randy ask me into a casual meeting a few weeks later. In this meeting, I was basically held against my will as Randy spouted off about everything on his mind, including Shane and the impending company bankruptcy. He told me that he thought we might need to get rid of Natalie, only because he didn't think that we could pay both her and myself while we went through it. Still not convinced that the bankruptcy would ever happen due to Randy's flighty behavior, I didn't put much thought into his suggestion. Once it hit me, I couldn't keep myself together. There was no way that I could do both jobs and get anything done on a weekly basis. Once that was brought up to me, I was upset and told Randy that there was no way I could do both jobs. I brainstormed on my feet for other alternatives, and the biggest one I came up with was reducing either my hours or the office hours completely. Since I made significantly more per hour than Natalie did, I threw myself under the bus in order to save her job. It was nice to have someone to talk to throughout the day over the past few months, and Natalie was someone. She helped me with anything excitedly, not batting an eyelash. I loved that about Natalie, and even in the short time I'd worked with her, knew that she had to remain a staple in the office. While not giving me an answer straight away (as per usual), Randy told me that he would take it under advisement and that we would find out about his decision when the time was right. The suggestion that I had made wasn't well thought out – I was not convinced I could finish everything with only thirty hours per week. At that point, however, I was more concerned with saving Natalie's job than keeping my pocketbook intact.

Mental exhaustion had begun to set in, and I did not know how much longer I could deal with this job and this life without completely losing it. There is nothing funny about working a job you hate, and this was the first one I had ever hated for good reason.

MAY 2009

From 12:01 AM on May 1, I was excited about taking my first-ever paid vacation to Columbus, Ohio for the Hell City Tattoo Convention at the end of the month. I was incredibly surprised when Randy signed off on the requested days no questions asked, and the forms were in my box when I arrived for work on the first. It was still a month away, but daydreaming had already begun. Stuck at the office alone on a Thursday morning, I was snapped back into the reality of how buried I was in work by the buzzer for the door downstairs. Natalie didn't come in until later, and she handled the new employee paperwork as one of her duties. I was immersed in accounting work (namely getting out monthly reports and getting ready for the week ending reports), and when I answered the buzzer, the employee told me that she was there to fill out paperwork.

"Do you have an appointment?"

"Yeah, at 2:30."

Looking at the clock, it read 10:00 AM.

"Nobody is here that can help you."

"But I got an appointment! I took the bus here."

"I'm sorry, but there is nobody here that can assist you. You need to come back at your appointment time."

In a huff, she turned around and left, figuring that I wasn't about to budge.

When Natalie arrived, I told her all about the tyrant I had encountered that morning, and we rolled our eyes collectively and returned to our usual duties. About five minutes after Natalie's arrival, the door buzzed again and it was the same employee. When she got upstairs, she claimed that the store's manager had given her the incorrect time and that she could not come back at 2:30. Instead of arguing with her, Natalie allowed her to do her paperwork. We both knew that she had taken the bus to the office and I did not want Natalie suffering the verbal abuse I had been at the receiving end of earlier.

We were wrong. Immediately after entering the office, the employee had an awful attitude, rudely asking Natalie why she hadn't been allowed to do her paperwork earlier and why she had been 'lied to' about the office being busy. Natalie informed her that she had only arrived a few minutes before, and had not yet been in the office when the woman initially buzzed. The employee, not believing her, went on a tirade, getting into Natalie's face and causing such a stir that I was forced to get up from what I was doing to ask what was going on in the waiting area. Once that happened, the employee got pretty quiet, but I could still hear her going at Natalie any chance that she got. When she was finally finished with her paperwork, she slammed the door on her way out of the office and Natalie showed up at my doorway mere moments later, eyebrows raised and asking what the hell had just happened. I told her that no matter what happened, she still needed to call the store and tell them that she had finished her paperwork, and regretfully, Natalie did just that.

During her conversation with the store's manager on duty, however, she was informed that the employee was incredibly rude to customers, and had even threatened violence against several of her coworkers during her last course of employment. The manager Natalie spoke to advised the store's general manager (her boss) not to hire the employee back, but he had and now there was nothing that could be done either way, or so we thought. Natalie asked me if I thought that an e-mail to Randy could be in order, and I told her that if she felt like writing one that she should.

She wrote the e-mail and sent it off to Randy. His reply was surprising, stating that she would not be rehired because of how she treated the office staff. Once Natalie received this message, I was surprised. She sent another asking for her name to not be brought up, and Randy stated that it was 'a little late for that'. His explanation for not rehiring her had been her treatment of the office staff, but he had not given names specifically. The employee only had contact with Natalie and I, so he really did not have to use them. Natalie was furious, and for good reason. She could see the girl coming back to the office to confront us. I did not care either way, since I could not see the employee returning just to make the situation worse. The unprofessional nature in which the situation had been handled had become commonplace for Randy, and there was nothing that he could do at this point that I could be surprised by. I told Natalie not to worry about it, and she informed me that she was still planning to lock the office each day when I wasn't around, just because she was nervous. I okay-ed it since I would have done the same thing, but told her not to let Randy know because of the hell storm I'd dealt with after my own near-miss back in November.

Only three weeks after I had suggested lowering my own office hours, Randy astounded both Natalie and I by deciding on one Thursday afternoon that he was going to reduce the hours of the entire office, with us now working only 11:30 AM-5:30 PM. He sent this via e-mail and said that any questions could be forwarded to him there. He stated that the regular hours would be resumed at summer's end. The only question that I had was when the new hours would start – seeing as it was pretty pertinent information. He replied to my question by stating that it would take place the following Monday. I had not thought much about the situation since I brought it up to Randy, figuring that he would forget about it as soon as he'd walked out of the room that April evening. I was still unsure of how I would do my entire job with my hours cut by ten per week, but I would have to figure out a way to consolidate accounting, unemployment, personnel, and my myriad of other responsibilities into a thirty-hour week. Natalie didn't mind, either, and this was a positive for her, since she had recently decided to go back to her second job at a retail store part-time. Many people would have been upset about this change, but I was okay with it. It meant that I would not have to spend as much of my workweek with my insufferable supervisors, and that I could have some time to myself and regain a social life. Doing calculations on the pay difference, I noticed that I would be making per week approximately what I was making before I was given my first increase. While Randy made it seem like the change was only because I had suggested it, I knew that it was his first way of trying to push me out... of course beside the fact that he never spoke to me unless he had to anymore. He was going to reduce my hours, and thus my pay, and he hoped that I would get sick of it and quit. Evaluating my options, I figured that I could either go and get another job, or grin and bear it. I chose the latter. I wanted to see how all of this would play out.

Since I started, one of my main focuses was the unemployment benefits that were paid out by the company. I was responsible for replying to all of the new separations, and handling the organization of any hearings that were called. Many of the separations never went to hearings, and we won approximately eighty percent of them. The other twenty percent was split between part-time employees who used unemployment benefits on a supplementary basis, and employees who had been unceremoniously fired for reasons thought up by Randy and Shane – reasons which never made sense to anyone but them, especially not from a legal standpoint. After the shock of actually having my hours reduced set in, I was questioned on two employees' unemployment benefits. The first was part-time, and the other had been getting benefits since September 2008, as he had been fired for an illegitimate reason. In the middle of May, I received two e-mails from Randy within two hours of one another asking why these two employees were getting unemployment benefits. I explained the situation several times, and rolled my eyes as I was questioned once more I just copied and pasted the same explanations into new e-mails. With the length of time that these employees had been receiving benefits, there was no way for us to lodge new appeals, and I explained that several times. Randy, who had no knowledge of unemployment, still thought that there was a way for us to get out of paying their benefits, and insisted on calling unemployment himself to get the same answer I had given him. Following that phone call, I was no longer questioned.

One other thing that hit me in the middle of the month was the fact that I had been employed by the franchise for one year. This year had been nothing like I thought it would be, and in reality, it all felt unbelievable. I never could have expected all of the things that transpired, and in a way it made me sick to realize that I had taken it for so long. I wanted to be doing something with my young life, not getting up every morning and going to an office to work for someone I hated more than anything. Everything seemed so simple when my employment started, and my job now was nothing like what it used to be. Every day felt like some sort of sick joke was being played on me, like there were cameras everywhere that I couldn't see and eventually all of my friends and family would jump out and scream "surprise!" Obviously, this was not in the cards for me. This was my real life. This was really my job.

Thankfully, things were quiet in the weeks leading up to my vacation. My roommate, Sam, and I had decided to move into a vacant apartment in the office's building at the suggestion of Jake, the building manager, and were set to move in early June. My vacation came up much faster than I expected it to, and soon I found myself on my way to Ohio, a good friend in tow and nothing to worry about. That is, until I got a phone call from the office late in the afternoon. It was Natalie.

"Liz, there is a huge argument happening in the office right now. Randy and Shane are in a meeting with Dylan (a general manager) and they are screaming at each other. I just heard furniture getting thrown around, Shane called Randy a faggot, and they are seriously yelling at each other right now. What do I do?"

"If you need to, I would leave the office for a few minutes and get your bearings straight, and go back when you feel comfortable. If anyone questions you, tell him or her to call me and I will stick up for you. That's bullshit, and you shouldn't have to deal with it."

When I hung up the phone, my friend wanted to know everything that had just happened. I was in such disbelief that there was nothing that I could say without sounding utterly and completely insane. Randy and Shane were now getting into altercations in the office during business hours and in front of store managers. All that I wanted to do was go into the office and ask the both of them what the fuck they were thinking – but it would have been looked down on by most people. I was helpless to give Natalie any other solace than telling her that what she was doing was right, and wondered in the back of my mind what could possibly come next. Wrestling in the conference room? Hair pulling suitable for the Jerry Springer stage? It didn't seem far off.

JUNE 2009

June didn't bring good things for our company whatsoever. The first week of the month, three of our twelve stores were closed due to poor sales. A new store had just opened in January, and the ball had been dropped from the word 'go'. Shane was supposed to be handling the opening of the store, and everything was done last minute from promotion to the build out of the space. That store, located in Racine, never made more than ten thousand dollars on a weekly basis. It hadn't even been open for six months, and it was a liability. The other two stores had been closed based on sales as well, but their issues were not as extreme. They had both been around for much longer, had established business, and didn't make as much as some others, but were in areas that other franchises would not deliver to. This didn't matter to Randy and Shane, who made the decision to close the stores amongst themselves and dropped the ball on that, too. None of the utilities had been shut off, from the phones to the electricity and gas, and we were still required to pay them until our keys were given back to the respective landlords and we were no longer liable. This, of course, was not taken care of by Randy or Shane. Randy had stopped paying rent on two of the stores in April because of poor sales, and the landlords had processed evictions, which were served on the entry door of the building one Friday afternoon early on in the month. Instead of taking them down when Natalie and I noticed them, we just left them there and wondered how long it would take Randy and Shane to notice. When we returned the next Monday, they were gone, so it had not taken them long.

Dealing with the floodgates opening to both customer and vendor complaints about the closed stores kept me busy. Natalie was still coming in every day and doing everything that she could to keep things running smoothly, and that same Monday she had put together a set of 500 menu box topper flyers for each store. This project had taken most of the day with our older-than-dirt copier, and was over 4,500 sheets of paper when completed. After spending the entire day on copies, she received an e-mail from Randy stating that he and Shane had decided to change the price on one of the coupons, so just to trash the flyers she'd made and create new ones. Randy asked her to just throw away an entire day of work and waste

4,500 sheets of paper. Since he was the boss, she did what he said, but it was still met with quite a bit of apprehension on her part.

While Randy was constantly calling in to bark orders to Natalie and I, we saw him less and less. On the afternoon of June 10th, I received a text message from my roommate, Sam.

"I love how there are a twenty one year old and a twenty three year old running Randy's office, and he is outside, busy detailing his moderately priced Acura."

From our personal apartment, we had a view of the parking lot from the balcony. Shortly after sending the text, I received a picture message that showed just that: Randy out in the parking lot, detailing his car. I told Natalie, and we soon found ourselves peering out the window in the conference room facing the parking lot, barely able to see for ourselves, but still with the ability to.

It was funny at first, but then when I got to thinking about it, it obviously meant that the company was not as important to Randy as he would have everyone think outwardly. Was this the reason for not getting answers to phone calls until after calling four or five times? Could he really be so self-involved that his business falling apart came secondary to his car? All signs pointed to yes. Of course neither of us would ever mention what we saw that afternoon, but it gave us a glimmering idea of just how Randy felt about his business while it crumbled before us.

With things still on edge between Randy and I, I was surprised when he pulled me into a meeting suddenly one afternoon. He asked me 'what my problem was lately', after bringing up some other business related items, and I told him flat-out.

"I don't feel like you genuinely want me here. You don't talk to me anymore unless you absolutely have to, and I feel like you treat me like a subhuman."

"I told you things would change in March."

"Change so drastically that you can't even speak to me one and one about business related matters? What sense does that make?"

"I told you things would change. I just want to see how you're feeling about things and where we should go from here."

"Randy, I just told you how I'm feeling. I don't enjoy my job or what I'm doing on a daily basis, and things are just made difficult by the fact that you're never around and only speak to me through e-mail. Do you want me here?"

"I don't know what you mean."

"It's simple. Do you want me here or not?"

"Liz, that's not an appropriate question."

"It is an appropriate question. I am treated awfully each and every day. You can't tell me that you still want me here treating me that way."

"You didn't answer my question."

"I have no problem with my position overall. It is outside influences that upset me and make it difficult to work on a daily basis. So no, I'm not happy if that's what you're asking. Do you want me here? That's all I want to hear you say."

"Liz, you constantly have a bad attitude. Natalie is so bubbly and nice and good to talk to, and lately you just… haven't been. You don't even say hello to me anymore."

"It is Natalie's job to be bubbly and nice, and it is now my job to crunch numbers. I say hello to you each and every day you come upstairs, but more often than not I find that you ignore me and go on to the next thing. Don't say that I don't say hello, because I do. That has nothing to do with this."

"I just want to see some improvement in your attitude. There is no reason for you to react so harshly and act like everything is such a big problem for you."

The entire meeting made absolutely no sense to me. Randy had wanted to "talk", but really all he had wanted to do was berate me and make me feel bad, which hadn't worked. Each and every day after that meeting when Randy and Shane came up the elevator into the office I did the best that I could to look over to them directly and say my hellos. It was the two of them that either didn't respond or walked right past me as if I wasn't there. I made no effort to talk to either of them or be nice to them anymore, because I had spent so much time being ignored and treated like shit that it just didn't make sense. They had formed their opinions on both

Natalie and myself, and it was obvious that Natalie was the new 'office princess'. It didn't bother me. Their approval didn't mean a thing to me, and if Randy thought that the meeting had scared me, it hadn't.

The other subject matter of the meeting had surprised me. Randy informed me that instead of putting the business into bankruptcy, he was intending to sell to either a group of investors or a single investor, and that depending on who bought the business, it would decide whether or not I was still employed. He also stated that the group of investors would be coming into town soon in the coming weeks to meet everyone and make a more full decision. He did not offer me an opportunity to ask questions about this, but I just took the information in and nodded and smiled, as I had done so many times before.

Randy's birthday had fallen on a weekend both years I had been employed for it, and I made an attempt to at least call him and wish him a happy birthday. This year, I opted for a text message instead of a phone call. Monday morning, I went to his favorite salon and got him a gift certificate for a haircut. Why would I waste the money on a gift for someone I could not stand? It was all about playing 'the game'. Randy informed me that it was the only gift he had received all year, and seemed genuinely surprised that I'd gotten him anything. For a guy who had Shane shoved so far up his ass on a regular basis, I was personally surprised that it was his only gift. Checkmate.

We were given very little notice of the impending visit from the investors. We were just told to make sure that the office was clean and presentable, and that we dressed up to impress them. Once they arrived, the show was on in full swing.

Each of them was an older gentleman, and each of them shook my hand and asked me questions about both myself and my history with the company, and did the same to Natalie. They asked me to pull some financials for them, which I did without a question or complaint, and I got the information they asked for very quickly. I overheard them tell Randy that I was a find, and smiled to myself. When Randy came up, I was expecting a train wreck, but he put his hand on my shoulder and just smiled, which I wasn't sure was a good or bad thing. He was putting on a show, just like Natalie and I were. The group was gone to tour stores just as soon as they'd arrived, and Natalie and I breathed a collective sigh of relief and went back to work.

One thing I wondered about the investors, however, was how much Randy had shared with them about Shane's history. Would they still be so gung ho about purchasing the company if they knew that an embezzler was second in command? There was no way they knew. Not that I would go and tell them, I just found it quite interesting to think about. There was no way that there were more businesspeople in the world that were as insane as Randy was.

Once we got through the investor experience, I thought that we would be right as rain for the beginning of July and the impending Independence Day holiday. Arriving to work on Monday the last week of the month, I was greeted by Natalie telling me that Randy had to speak with me immediately, and groaned as I set the paychecks down on her desk and headed down to Randy's apartment. As I had been doing every Monday for over a year, I went to the payroll company's office and then proceeded to go to the bank for Randy to deposit his paycheck. He knew this, had always known this, and it had somehow slipped his mind.

As I stood in front of Randy's apartment door and knocked, I heard Shane come to the other side.

"It's Liz, should I let her in?"

And the door was unlocked. I really wanted to tell Shane that I could hear everything that he'd just said through the door, but decided against it and headed into Randy's office to see what he needed. In reality, what he needed wasn't any sort of emergency situation – he had only wanted to give me some paperwork such as bills and bank statements, and apparently found the one floor trip to be too great to attempt. While I was walking back upstairs with my inch-high stack of paperwork, I was sure that I had to be going crazy. Nobody was that forgetful, nor that lazy, and certainly would not have made such a huge deal out of something so miniscule.

Mondays had been so bad in recent weeks that I had coined them 'Choke-N-Strangle Mondays', and for good reason. There was never a Monday that I could go through stress free. There was always invented drama or invented deadlines, and many times I found myself thinking I was going crazy because of them.

I was called late in the afternoon on the same Monday as the payroll incident to be told that the expository tax had not been paid for the quarter, and that it was 'halting the sale of the business'. I had never received the tax form from the state. These forms always came in the mail in advance of the due date. I told Randy that the expository tax hadn't been paid because I had never received the paperwork due to his having the mail key, and that I needed it to complete the calculations. Ignoring the bit about me needing the paperwork to complete the calculations, he all but demanded he have the calculations by that afternoon. So I did the next best thing to having the original paperwork: I Googled it.

Coming up with the tax form was not difficult, nor was doing the calculations with the form I downloaded. I printed the form and both faxed and e-mailed it to Randy, only for him to tell me that he didn't think the calculations were right and wanting me to go over them a second time. I had done all of the calculations based on the sales for that quarter, based off of sales that I had downloaded from our system, and there were no errors. I found myself explaining this for over ten minutes, with Randy still giving me dead silence on the other end of the phone before giving up and stating that I would have a check for the amount any minute.

Thinking that there was no way that Randy could possibly screw me over any more in one day; I was not surprised to receive another asinine e-mail from Randy. He stated that he needed me to come in at 10 AM the next day, in order to participate in "a conference call regarding accounting issues." Of course I wasn't told which issues these were or given any opportunity to prepare myself for the meeting at hand, but figured that I would grin and bear it, doing the best that I could.

The next morning, I got up early and headed to the office for the 10 AM start time of the call. I waited until 10:30 before texting Randy and asking him what was taking so long and why I hadn't been called to be included in this conference call as of yet. He stated that they no longer needed me, and that I could go and come back. I was absolutely floored. Not that I wasn't awake already, but it was just the fact that he had me come in early and expected me not to ask questions when there was no call at 10:00 AM to participate in.

'Choke-N-Strangle Tuesday' was becoming a real possibility this week. After I left and came back at my normal time that same day, I worked and was taking a brief break as Natalie came in to find me.

"Guess what?"

"What?"

"We're working at Glendale Days on Thursday and Friday!" She mused sarcastically.

"You have got to be fucking kidding me."

Glendale Days is a yearly Independence Day celebration where there are carnival rides, food vendors, and things of the sort. Glendale Days was also the location of Shane's 'accident' the year before. As a vendor, we had a pizza trailer that we brought out and would sell pizza from. The pizza was delivered from a local store several times a day, and was sold with tickets instead of money. When Natalie told me that Randy and Shane were planning to have us work Glendale Days the last two days of the week, I thought that it was a joke. We had just closed three stores as a franchise, some employees were struggling to find hours at the stores we still had open, and they were going to close the office for two days so that their office staff could sell pizzas out of a fucking trailer? It made no sense to me whatsoever, but I decided that if they wanted to pay me three times what they paid a typical store employee, that I would not complain. I did complain, however, when I was told that the hours for the first day would be 9:00 – 6:00, and the hours for the second day were unknown as of yet.

The fact that I had to work in a trailer and sell pizza just got a lot more annoying. What kind of festival would expect their vendors there at 8:30 in the morning? What kind of Independence Day event started at 8:30 in the morning? I knew that there had to be a mistake, and would have to wait until the days of the festival themselves to figure out the answers to my questions.

I continued to think, naively, that things would get better. That perhaps I would wake up from this nightmare one day, pinch myself, and none of this would be real. I knew that even I could not get that lucky, and just wondered how much longer this company could stay afloat. Sure, we had the new investors and that was supposed to cure everything, but we had dumb and dumber at the helm, and all that I knew through my mother's advice was that "you can't fix stupid". That quote ran through my head almost constantly while I dealt with all of this. There was no way to rationalize this, because this was absolutely insane. I didn't know what to do or where to head anymore, and it was getting more and more difficult to take.

JULY 2009

There was nothing special about July first from the get-go except for our annual health insurance renewal meeting. The renewal meeting itself had been a disaster. It was our insurance agent, Randy, Shane, and myself. In 2008, the meeting had only been with Randy and myself, but since Shane seemed to be a part of everything lately, walking into the meeting and seeing him there didn't surprise me in the least. The renewal meeting was standard, with our agent going over our current plan in comparison with some others that he took the time to look into, as well as the going rates for each. The information was well laid-out in spreadsheet format, and was very easy to understand. Throughout the meeting, however, Randy stopped the agent in order to ask where we were, or what page we were even looking at. He was too interested in his iPhone or his laptop to actually pay attention to what was going on. Due to that fact, the company was then relegated to a policy with a deductible $250 over what the last year's policy was, only because the monthly cost was one hundred dollars less than the current plan. Many times throughout the meeting I was reduced to burying my head in my hands due to embarrassment, and mouthing apologies to our insurance agent for Randy's inability to pay attention to something so simple as a fifteen-minute insurance renewal.

After saying our goodbyes to the insurance agent, Randy asked me to join him and Shane in the conference room. I grabbed my notepad (a staple for these types of meetings), and headed in, with no preconceived notions about what the meeting could be about. Randy stated that he had received a text message from Nicki; the manager who Shane was sleeping with stating that I was telling the store managers that Randy is gay. After Randy had come out to me many months earlier, I had never told a soul at the company. This was something I held in very high regard as far as trust, and no matter what my feelings about Randy were at any given time I never would have done that. I had many homosexual friends, and the thought of outing one of them without their knowledge would never cross my mind.

After the words had come out of his mouth, I was absolutely flabbergasted. I could not believe that Randy would actually believe that I would do something like that. I looked right into his eyes and told him that

I had never spoken a word of the conversation in question to anyone, and that I thought it was asinine for it to even come together in the form of a meeting. Obviously, I was angry, and tried to stay objective but it was difficult. Once I told Randy that I had never breathed a word to anyone, he believed me. My eyes had never once diverted from his, and my honesty came out in each and every one of my words. Attempting to keep myself sane was very difficult when Shane piped in, stating that we should speak to the other store managers to see whom else I had told. I absolutely could not believe the balls it must have taken the two of them to put together a meeting for something so insane.

If they wanted me gone, they almost got their wish that afternoon. When I was finally released from the meeting, I slammed the conference room door and left the office for a good twenty-minute release in my own apartment. This included a yelling and screaming tangent, to express the anger I was obviously feeling. At this point, I had two choices: I could either go upstairs, grab my things, and leave, or go back upstairs and prove that I hadn't done anything by continuing to work as usual. Thinking more about 'the game', I realized that if I left I would be giving Randy and Shane everything they wanted. They wanted to do something to make me quit, so that they would not have to deal with firing me and having to deal with unemployment.

Opting for neither, I went back upstairs after twenty minutes and was met by Natalie and Randy in the front area of the office, Randy asking Natalie to text me and tell me to come back. Since he no longer had to do that, he called me into another meeting in the conference room. In that meeting it was just he and I with Shane nowhere to be found, and he told me that he didn't understand where my anger came from. He thought that there was no reason for me to be angry if there was no truth to the allegations against me, and I had to spend at least ten minutes explaining each and every reason why I was upset to a man who could not have seemed to care less. Once he got that out of the way he began to talk all about how he was intending on 'pressuring weak managers to leave', essentially by forcing them into quitting. Tim, our former area supervisor turned store manager was one, and Dylan had also quit recently due to not wanting to be surrounded by the drama anymore. Neither of them was shoved out – both of them just got sick of the constant flurry of negative energy and rumors. Really, I didn't care what Randy and Shane's plans were. I was just more floored at the fact that Randy would see that I was incredibly upset and flip the situation back around so that it would be on him all over again. It made me sick. He made me sick.

The day after the meeting was the first day that Natalie and I were working the Glendale Days festival. I woke up at 8:00 AM, showered, and got dressed to work, exchanging a few text messages with Natalie as I was planning to pick her up after running up to the office for the trailer keys. At 9:00 AM, I received a text message from Randy. 'Call me.' So I picked up the phone and did as he asked.

"Hello?"

"You texted?"

"You and Natalie don't need to work the Glendale Days event today. I just wanted to let you know."

"Oh, okay."

And the call was over just as soon as it had begun, thanks to Randy hanging up. After climbing back into bed, I called Natalie.

"Hey, guess what?"

"What?"

"I just got a phone call from Randy, apparently we don't have to work Glendale Days today."

"Are you fucking kidding me?"

"Nope."

"Ugh. See you at 11:30."

"I know, right? See you then."

Later, we found out that the event didn't start until 4 PM that day, and that we had both gotten up far earlier than we normally would have for no reason whatsoever. I struggled to get back to sleep, and peeled myself out of bed to go upstairs about ten minutes late, being met at the door by a Natalie who hadn't been able to get back to bed, and who was still frustrated over the events of that morning. We did what we could to make the best of a bad situation, however, and were thankful for the fact that we barely saw hide or hair of Randy and Shane for most of the day.

Due to the impending Independence Day holiday, the manager payroll which was typically sent in on Friday needed to be sent in on Thursday so that we would still receive checks the following Monday. I told Randy several times both via phone and e-mail that this was necessary, and he never got the message. At 4:45 PM, Randy called the office and asked Natalie to tell me that I needed to bring the manager payroll out to the Glendale Days event, which was approximately fifteen minutes from the office. Nothing could be easy for me that day and I ran into almost forty five minutes of traffic both due to the time of day and road construction that left me with a less-than-stellar attitude. Once I arrived with the payroll, I was questioned once again why it was necessary to be sent that day, and was finally released after I had explained it to Randy a fourth time. After arriving back at the building, I opted not to go back up to the office since it was close enough to my end time to not even be worth it, and the payroll was input just as it was supposed to be, although at the last possible moment. At 9:30 PM, I received a text message from Randy stating that I was responsible for working the event the next morning at 9:30. Groaning, I set my alarm for an early wake up, and reluctantly went to bed early to compensate.

Getting up early the next morning was hellacious. With one eye open, I grabbed a Monster out of our refrigerator, went upstairs to grab the trailer keys, list of duties, and a windbreaker embroidered with the company logo, and headed on my way. Though I was barely awake, I made it to the park in one piece, though had to drive around for nearly twenty minutes to find an open entrance. Figuring that the day would be boring, I went prepared with a book of word searches and the current book I was reading, and was looking forward to a day of doing nothing but sitting around.

Setting up the trailer wasn't difficult – it involved lifting a flap and putting in a couple of pins to steady it, as well as plugging the power supply cord into a power box outside. My only issue had been my height. I wasn't tall or strong enough to get the flap up on my own. Though I struggled, I opted to wait for the girl who was working with me – an assistant manager from one of our stores – to arrive so that she could help me. Several people came up and asked when we would start selling food once our first delivery arrived at 10 AM, and unfortunately for them, the ticket booths didn't open until 11:30. Since we were selling food-using tickets instead of money, there was nothing we could do until the booths opened. So, we sat and did word searches, and the first food we handed out had been in the warmer for over an hour and a half. The day wasn't stressful, and had actually been relaxing (or at least as relaxing as a day of sitting in a pizza trailer with nothing to do can be). That was until Randy and Shane showed up at about 5:00 PM. I was told that my shift would be from 9:30 to 5:30, and when they arrived I was looking forward to the possibility of heading home early on a Friday afternoon. Of course, nothing could go my way, and the two of them were too busy with setting up Randy's laptop (which yes, he brought everywhere), and even when I asked Randy if I could leave at 5:30, he told me that I needed to ask Shane. Shane was busy with Randy's laptop speaker setup for about a half hour, and at 6:00 he asked if I needed anything because he and Randy were planning to check out the festival.

"Um, can I go home?"

"Oh yeah, yeah. Have a good weekend!" He spoke as I handed him the keys.

I could not complain. I made almost ten dollars for wasting that extra half hour.

For as bad as I thought working the pizza trailer would be, it really wasn't. I had a pretty decent day, getting to know an assistant manager I had barely any interaction with, and I was happy overall with how everything worked out.

Things were quiet at the beginning of the next week as well, until Jake, the property manager, e-mailed me early in the morning on Tuesday to ask me if I had spoken to Randy. I told him that no, I hadn't, and asked what it was regarding. Apparently, there had been several police calls to Randy's apartment the night before for noise complaints, and that he had been up since 3:00 AM dealing with both the angry residents and the police because of it. Several of the calls had been for noise, and one was even for a domestic disturbance. I went downstairs to ask him for some more information, and he told me that Randy had received a noise ticket the night before for a party he'd thrown. As we could put it together, the party had been Randy, Shane, and Nicki. Shane got drunk and fought with Randy, who locked himself in the bathroom like many a fourteen-year-old girl at a high school party. Still drunk, Shane had also thrown his own iPhone off of Randy's thirteenth floor deck. All day, Randy and Shane were not answering their phones, and Randy even missed an appointment with our advertising representative. After making several phone calls to Randy and Shane, Shane finally returned one stating that Randy 'had the flu' and that his own 'phone broke'. Sure, if 'having the flu' means having a wicked hangover and having a 'broken phone' means throwing his own phone off of the balcony. With eye rolls abounding, I found solace in knowing that Randy wasn't dead and that the drama would live to see yet another day.

Our office attire was business casual. In any typical office, black or colored jeans would be acceptable on a daily basis, as long as they weren't full of holes or awful looking. While most days I wore dress pants, some days I dressed down and wore black jeans with my typical outfits of button-down shirts and sweaters. My choice of wardrobe had come under fire several times in the last six months, with the first time being in December, the second time being in April, and the third time being in the middle of July. On the day in question, I wore a pair of nice black jeans, a green t-shirt, and a black cardigan. My arms and legs were covered, and I was wearing dress shoes. That particular day, I was asked to go to the manager meeting to deliver some supplies from the office, and returned back to an e-mail from Randy. The e-mail stated that the office staff would be required to wear the store general manager's uniform of a green polo shirt emblazoned with the company logo, khaki pants, hat or visor, and black shoes. I told him many times that I did not feel comfortable with this and didn't think that it was appropriate, but it was never taken into advisement. Randy's only reaction was always "it's comfortable", and could never give any other reason besides. The rest of the e-mail stated that he no longer wanted to deal with 'general managers asking why I was allowed to wear jeans and a t-shirt to work when they were required to wear uniforms'. Just to cover my bases, I texted one of the managers that was at the meeting and asked if anything had been discussed, and he stated that nothing had been brought up in the meeting and that there had been no one on one time. Knowing this, I asked Randy for the opportunity to meet and discuss, and he refused to hold a meeting or discuss anything with me. This just seemed like another way to get me upset enough to leave, and as I grabbed my green polo shirt out of the uniform closet, I attempted to decide what my next play would be. This was all a game, after all.

While Natalie was upset about the abrupt change in uniform mostly because it involved buying new clothes, I told her not to worry about it and to keep doing what she was doing. I knew that the uniform change was just to upset me, and had my own plans as far as how I could make it work for me. The biggest part of that plan was yes, I would wear the required uniform, but I would wear some of the most obnoxious, brightly colored makeup I could muster finding out of my makeup case. This play I coined 'Operation Glamotage'. I did what they asked, wearing the uniform, but if anything was mentioned about my makeup in the right context, I could claim sexual harassment and quit without a question of being able to receive unemployment. The first day, I chose to wear blue and teal eye shadow, and a shade of lipstick called 'Backstage Bambi', a fluorescent pink reminiscent of all things 80's. Though it wasn't mentioned in a negative way, Randy noticed the lipstick right away and I just claimed to have found it and wanted to wear it. They were playing right into my hands, and I couldn't imagine it going any better. With the right situation, I knew that it had already gotten under his skin. Each day, it got a little bit more obscene, with the addition of another obnoxious color or glitter eyeliner. I was disappointed when Randy never mentioned it again, and eventually gave up, going back to my plain face, with eyeliner and mascara on a day when I was feeling especially energetic in the morning.

Shortly after 'Operation Glamotage' came and went, Natalie sent me a text a good hour before I was supposed to be in one day. 'You have to see this.' Like anyone who enjoys a good story, I headed upstairs to the office immediately after receiving the text, and was greeted by Natalie who could barely contain her laughter at a customer complaint that had come in.

This complaint wasn't from a customer at all. We deduced that it was from an employee with an assumed name, and it went into the way the company was run, using negative terms for both Randy and Shane, and ending with the classiest term I have ever read: "PS – Shane and Randy suck each other." As soon as I read it, I knew I had to have a copy, so I made one and brought it back downstairs with me. Before I arrived back to the office for work, Randy had snapped up the original copy (which had come through the fax machine like every other complaint, and ostensibly e-mailed to him as well), muttering something about how it had to be a former employee trying to get a rise out of him. While I didn't believe that aspect for a second, I just laughed at the fact that Randy thought that everyone around him was so stupid that nobody would see things that were actually happening.

There were still constant rumors flying about how much time Shane and Randy spent together, and I routinely saw Shane driving away from the building from anywhere between midnight to 4 AM. There wasn't only work happening during their time together, and you would have to be an idiot to think so. The rumors had gone from Shane answering Randy's door in his pajamas to the two of them getting so drunk one weekend that they had wound up touching each other and Shane had wound up flipping out. I never received confirmation one way or another, and the truth was I really didn't want to know what happened behind closed doors with the two of them. All that I wanted was to come in to work every day, collect my paychecks, and leave at the end of the week with some semblance of a clear head. Any sane person would want that, at least.

The new uniform policy only stayed in effect for a week. Randy saw that I didn't like it, and decided that pushing it would only make things worse for our already strained relationship. He constantly told me that I had a bad attitude and that he could not understand why I acted the way I did, but also seemed to forget that my bad attitude was because of the way I was being treated on a daily basis. During the same time he told me about the uniform policy, Randy also told me that if I continued to assist in assembling things for the transition to the new ownership in a month, that I would receive a cash bonus when all was said and done. I did not expect that to happen as far as I could throw it, but it was still something to think about. I couldn't help but wonder if he would actually follow through, though I was not expecting him to.

Personal property taxes for each store for 2008 were due by the end of March, but weren't taken care of until the food licenses came up for renewal in June. All of the personal property taxes had been sent to collections, though I had told Randy from the day they were due on that they were required to be paid. The only time that this mattered to him was when the food licenses were overdue, and we were being threatened with store closures if they weren't paid by the end of the month. Two days before month's end, I received an e-mail from Randy wanting to know the calculations for both the personal property taxes and food licenses for each store. I e-mailed him the information, and was surprised to receive signed checks the next day, which I mailed out. Hours after mailing out the checks, I received another e-mail from Randy asking how many checks I needed for the personal property taxes and licenses. These were checks that he had signed hours, if not a day earlier, and he somehow completely forgot about their existence. I told him that the checks were already signed and mailed, and the subject was dropped. This would not stop the municipalities from closing us down if they felt the time was right, but at least I knew I had done my part with the constant reminders leading up to the actual receipt date. While I was confused by Randy's reactions, I also could not help but laugh. He must have been on drugs; either that or he was losing his mind completely. And honestly? I thought I'd lost mine many months earlier for staying in this job.

AUGUST 2009

The change of ownership transition date, I learned, was to be August 24th. This would be the date that my position would no longer be necessary within the company, and I was left with question marks in place of firm answers whenever I questioned Randy in regards to anything big or small. Those were not our only problems. There was an increasing amount of tension building between Randy and Shane, tension that came to a head within the first three days of the month with yet another screaming match in the office while I was out.

When Natalie gave her two-week notice, I wasn't surprised. She had stated back in May that if another altercation such as the furniture-shoving gay-bashing argument happened, that she was out. She was not going to put herself in a risky situation at work, and I truly could not blame her for her feelings. I did what I could to convince her to work out her two-week notice, even though she questioned me every day as to whether or not she should come in the next day. The only reason that she stayed as long as she did was for my own benefit and nothing else. I had so much to do until the transition date almost a month away, and she didn't want to leave me in a worse situation than she had to. At this point, when she left I would be saddled down with not only my accounting responsibilities, but all of the former responsibilities that she'd taken over on the administrative side of things. Even answering the phone took a load off my shoulders, and I figured that I would have two weeks to figure out how I would handle things without her. I could not have been more wrong.

Three days after giving her two-week notice, I received a text message from Natalie stating that she had decided not to fulfill her two weeks, and that she was inputting the weekly payroll and leaving. By time I got the text message, she was already gone, and she informed me that she had also e-mailed Randy to let him know of her decision not to fulfill her two-week commitment. Unfortunately, the e-mail never arrived, as Randy's e-mail had been a bit buggy for the last several days. Once I arrived, I called to let Randy know what was going on, and he was immediately upstairs to ask me why Natalie had left and why she had not wanted to fulfill her two weeks. I played dumb and told him I had no idea, not making any mention of the altercation that had forced her decision earlier in the week. I was not about to get involved in the rumor mill that was commonplace in the company - I had learned from experience that it was a dangerous place to be.

With the sting of Natalie's departure barely settled in, I was excited to finally be done for the week, looking forward to putting out some resumes as I truly had no idea how much longer my employment would last. I was surprised when Randy once again entered my office at 5:30 PM, when payroll was supposed to be sent in for guaranteed Monday pickup, and when I was supposed to leave. He stated that he needed to add a bonus to his paycheck.

"The payroll is done, and it needs to be sent in as soon as possible otherwise it may not be ready for Monday and that would be a problem."

"It will just have to be a problem."

"How much is the bonus?"

"Eighteen thousand."

I couldn't even hide my surprise at the amount he'd told me.

"How much?"

"Eighteen thousand."

That seemed like a little more than a regular bonus. The largest bonus I had ever entered throughout my tenure at the company was five hundred dollars. This smelled fishier than a brand new can of Chicken of the Sea. Randy told me that it was less of a bonus and more of a gift from the company's current investor, so that he would have the appropriate amount of money to buy his share of the business when investments changed hands.

Since Randy was my boss, I couldn't exactly say no, but the circumstances surrounding this 'bonus' weren't adding up. He assured me that he had the blessing of the company's current investor, although I had no way to verify such as I was never allowed contact with him myself. Regretfully, I entered the bonus.

"How much is it with taxes included?"

The full bonus was taken down significantly with the addition to his almost $2,000 weekly salary. If entered with his current tax exemptions, half of the bonus would have gone to taxes alone.

"Enter it without taxes."

Yet again, my jaw dropped. But I did what he told me to, because he was my boss and I couldn't very well show that type of insubordination. As awful as I felt about the possibility of my boss taking almost twenty thousand dollars from the company without anything in writing as verification, I was thrown yet another curveball.

Randy wanted to then meet with me to discuss my future with the company after the new investors took over on the 24th. Knowing that I had already been at work a half hour longer than I should have been, I figured 'what the hell' and said that if he wanted to do it, we could do it right then.

What I found out in this meeting was that all of my current job functions were being outsourced to the corporate office. From the beginning of the meeting on, Randy tore into me regarding my negative attitude.

"You have a bad attitude."

"I have a bad attitude because you treat me like I have a disease."

"That's not true, Liz. You're making things up."

"How can I make up the fact that you don't talk to me unless you absolutely have to? You have even called Natalie on accounting issues."

"Would you want to talk to you? Natalie is so happy and bubbly, and you just aren't."

"Am I supposed to be after all of this?"

"After all of what?"

"What you guys have been putting me through since March."

"I don't know what you're talking about."

This meeting seemed less informational and more like a personal attack the longer it went on. Yes, communications between Randy and I had broken down, but not through any fault of my own. Randy had been avoiding speaking to me personally as if I did have some sort of communicable disease, especially since Natalie had come on board. He was constantly making reference to my 'change in attitude', though there was none to report. I still called him at least once a day, even if I didn't need anything and just to see if he wanted to talk, because that was how our relationship had developed. I knew that it wasn't entirely healthy, but I also knew that he surrounded himself with 'friends' that he paid, Shane as a prime example.

Speaking of Shane, Randy also stated that he believed my issues with

Shane came down to my being jealous of the relationship that the two of them shared. Whether or not it was sexual, it was wildly unhealthy, and I couldn't see any sane person being jealous of a dysfunctional homosexual work relationship. At that point, I tuned him out for the remainder of our 45-minute meeting.

For a meeting that was supposed to tell me what my future with the company was, I was no closer to an answer than I had been at the start. Once 7 PM rolled around, I was finally allowed to leave the office for the weekend. I couldn't have been happier to at that point. With everything else going on, the extra hour and a half at work had not been a good one.

The drama couldn't wait long once I arrived back into the office the next Monday morning. No sooner had I arrived than Randy snapped up his check stub, making his bonus smell even fishier. Over the weekend, I received an e-mail from Randy indicating that Shane would be receiving a $100 weekly pay increase. It seemed like only weeks before a $125 weekly payback was removed from Shane's checks for the money he'd stolen. Now, Shane would be pulling in an additional $5200 yearly, and I hadn't seen any improvement in his work since I'd started. If anything, it deteriorated the longer their destructive relationship continued. Shane did less and less, and Randy commended him more and more. Shortly after this, Shane arrived to the office with a shiny new Mac Book Pro. I knew from what Randy had told me that Shane didn't have enough pocket money to afford a $2500 computer, but who was I to judge? That was probably just my faux jealousy and not actual common sense – it seemed that nobody else at the company knew what common sense was.

As the days progressed into a couple more weeks, I constantly prodded Randy for more information on the transition and what my role would be. He always stated that we would meet, but never set anything in stone, until the 25th (the day after the transition to my knowledge). In this meeting, he informed me that the transition was being pushed back three weeks to September ninth. This gave me a bit of relief in knowing I would continue to have stability, but I was also amidst a feeling of dread at having to prolong my employment for three more weeks.

Instead of tearing me down in this meeting as he had in so many before, Randy stated that he was going to speak to the new investors about putting me into some form of marketing role, though he had no specifics. Once again, to get my answers I would have to wait for yet another meeting, and he had no idea what the date of that meeting would be or when he would have further information. A bit of a shaky leg to stand on, but I had to take what I was given and roll with the punches. I was still filing resumes with other companies, and tried to have some form of plan in place in case there wasn't another job available. While this meeting had given me a small amount of information about my future with the new company, I still had nothing set in stone and had to cultivate other options.

While not directly affecting me, as August progressed I noticed an influx of new supplies being shipped to the office and needing to sign for far more packages than I was used to. Most of them were from Dell Computers, and a few were from the corporate office in the form of uniforms and other office supplies. When entering my weekly accounting numbers, I noticed that the stores had begun ordering three times their usual food amounts. While I yet again had no way to confirm or deny this with anyone higher than Randy, I had a feeling that Randy and Shane were stockpiling food in the stores and high-dollar computer equipment before the money tree ran dry and they could no longer run amok in the way they had been. By the end of the month, I also found out that the bonus that Randy had been given was half of the necessary $45,000 for him to buy into his own share of the new company. While I didn't agree with his ways and means of getting the money, I could see why he would need that much that fast. Through my weeks of depositing Randy's paycheck for him, I found out via his deposit slips that he ran through his $2,000 weekly paychecks as if they were bottles of mineral water, and had shopped himself broke by the next week. Not such great tactics for someone who was supposed to be such a great businessman. Of course, I knew at this point that I wasn't working for a great businessman – I was working for a crook and a liar.

Randy's crooked nature never directly affected me until the end of August. As a company, Randy rented three parking spaces in the outdoor surface parking lot of the building where the office was housed. We did not pay for these spots, but instead would give the office pizza whenever they needed it for meetings or special days. Due to some vandalism that took place over the weekend in question, Jake, the property manager, wanted to order pizza to thank some outside cleaning personnel. Jake e-mailed Randy and I and I called him to confirm his order. After receipt, I also called Randy.

"Yes?"

"Just calling to see if you want me to take care of Jake's pizza order."

"What pizza order? No, they aren't getting pizza."

Jake had ordered pizza many times throughout my employment, and had never once been denied by Randy.

"Why not? Is something going on?"

"No. If Jake has questions, he can ask me." Click.

That led to my having to call Jake with the bad news. When he asked why Randy had opted not to give him pizza, I did not have a straight answer for him. Not only did Randy have a deal with Jake for the pizza, but they had signed a contract. This contract extended to the end of the lease on the apartment we rented, and in laymen's terms was pizza for parking spaces. Both Randy and Jake had signed their names to it, and Randy had inexplicably opted not to fulfill his end of the deal with their contract. This left Jake in a predicament of needing to feed these people. I told him that if he wanted, I would still give him free pizza cards to take care of lunch. He denied and opted to call in an order from a competitor, as well as e-mailing Randy to let him know that due to Randy's not holding up his end of their contract, he would no longer be allowed to use the surface parking spaces outside.

While I used one of the spaces while I was at work and often moved my car back out to the street for the night, I figured it would be nice to have one of them to use all the time. I e-mailed Jake and asked if I could have one of the newly opened spaces in exchange for me doing some cleaning and other necessities around the building versus having to pay. He agreed, and though I was supposed to take possession of my parking space on September first, this issue made it so that I could take possession about a week early.

Once Randy realized that I had one of his former parking spaces, however, he was not happy. He told me that I was no longer allowed to speak to Jake, and proceeded to send Jake a barrage of e-mails about how he had violated the contract by allowing me to take the space. Had he forgotten about his refusal to feed the office only days before? Randy's e-mails to Jake were full of threats of legal action over giving me a parking space, though he would not have a legal leg to stand on. One afternoon, Randy came into my office.

"I need you to write a statement about your conversation with Jake over the parking spaces."

"What do you mean? We only discussed his pizza order and not the parking spaces."

"I am planning to discuss the contract with my lawyer and I need you to write a statement about your conversation."

The fact that Randy wanted me to write a statement floored me. There was nothing to it except for things that Randy did to violate his own contract, and I was not about to write down a personal agreement I had with my landlord over a parking space. That was what Randy wanted. Instead of ruffling more feathers, I wrote the statement. In it, I mentioned nothing about my deal with Jake, as it was none of Randy's business and had to do with my own lease. I faxed it to Randy just as he asked me to, and never heard about it again. I made sure to sign and fax the handwritten original, so that there was no way he could write something additional or put my signature on another document. I truly could not believe that it had to go this far, and also did not believe that Randy would be able to go to a lawyer with a straight face and tell this story.

The fact that I had a parking space did not bother Randy. The part that bothered him was the fact that it was one of *his former* spaces. I did not mind Randy's upset - it just showed that when he did not get his way, he would act like a child. He always wanted things to go his way, and if they didn't he would do everything that he could to ensure there was hell to pay.

The end of August brought me a strange peace amongst the chaos of Randy versus Jake. I could finally see the light at the end of the tunnel, although I was hoping it was a bit closer than it was in reality. Seeing the 24th come and go had been a disappointment, but I could finally see my out coming, and I was fully intending on taking advantage of what I could – any sane person would.

SEPTEMBER 2009

September barely got off to a proper start before the drama started all over again. All I knew walking in on September first was that the company changed hands on the ninth and I still had no information. I received a phone call from one of our assistant managers the afternoon of the first stating that at that day's assistant manager meeting, Randy and Shane had referred to the new office as their own, not mentioning me. One of the managers piped up and attempted to bring my role up, but the subject was changed immediately.

While I would not have minded driving to the new office site, it bothered me that there was constant reference to it that I was not included in. The new investors had decided to move the office from its' current location in a $2500 monthly penthouse apartment to the basement of the 'home store', and things had been in action for the move for some time. Of course, I had been given no information whatsoever. It did not bother me, though – the less I knew, the less I could be held accountable for if the company ever did fold and I was ever questioned.

As the date of the transition got closer, my duties lessened further and further. On September seventh, instead of a weekly meeting, the store's general managers were instructed to pick their checks up at the office. I wasn't told, only found out when the first arrived. I was used to this being pretty common practice, so just called Randy to verify that I could release the checks and did so. I called him mid-afternoon and told him that I was going downstairs to retrieve the day's mail, and came back upstairs only to find that the checks were gone.

I checked both the main door and my office door, and the main door had been locked and my office door had been closed. Confused, I called Randy. He informed me that he had come up and taken the checks, but did not offer me any further information. He told me to call him when any managers arrived, and that he would bring their checks up himself. This was all fine and good, but every manager that came in after that point had to wait upwards of twenty minutes for their checks, even though Randy was just one floor away, and only seconds via elevator.

Having the managers in the office was something that Randy dreaded, because he knew that I would strike up short conversations with them and find out things he didn't want me to. On this particular day, I found out that there had been a 'farewell barbecue' at his apartment that past Saturday, a barbecue I had not been informed about, much less invited to. That was my first inclination as to both how much I meant to the company as well as what my future would be.

Prior to the weekend, I sent Randy an e-mail asking if we could meet to discuss my future with the company. It seemed like I was a broken record at this point, but I needed to know because I needed to know if my schedule would change, as well as needing to know if I was going to need to continue searching for other employment. The e-mail was never replied to, but Randy poked his head into my office on the seventh to tell me that we would talk on the afternoon of the eighth. Of course, the meeting on the afternoon of the eighth never happened.

Nearly two weeks had passed in September thus far, and things changed. My workload was reduced by about eighty percent, and I had trouble keeping myself busy throughout most days. One major change I saw was that I was seeing the store's managers more and more, and that they were bringing large amounts of cash up to the office for Randy and Shane. This was in lieu of depositing them to the bank, and it was a bit fishy to me that there was that much money going into the hands of not only someone responsible for the theft of $40,000 in Shane, but someone who obviously had his own monetary issues in Randy. I kept my feelings silent, however, and collected the deposits and gave them to Randy without a word about how uneasy I felt. It was not good to have that kind of money in the office, I understood, and above all really didn't trust either of them as far as I could throw them.

The week came and went. Ironically, on Friday the 13th I questioned Randy yet again as to when we would discuss my future with the company. He asked me when I would be home over the weekend, and I told him, only breaking my 'no contact on weekends' rule because I needed to know what to expect. He told me he would call or text me when he had time.

That of course didn't happen, and whenever I texted him I was informed that he was too busy.

On the evening of Sunday the 15th, I finally received a text to say that if I could be out to the new office in a half hour, that our meeting could take place. At this point, it was 7:30 PM on a Sunday, and as much as I didn't want to go, I needed to.

I was greeted with anything but smiles when I arrived to the office. I was sat out in the reception area and told that Randy and Shane would be with me soon, sighing to myself and thinking that I would have to deal with the Randy and Shane Show for the inevitable event of my either not having a job, or being offered a job that was completely unlike anything I had experience with.

Just like my first interview, I waited approximately twenty minutes for my meeting. Shane emerged from the conference room, telling me that Randy would be with me in moments, and went back upstairs to the restaurant. Randy was in the conference room for another five minutes before finally coming to get me and beginning our meeting.

"I know you aren't going to like the position."

"What is it?"

"Marketing at a rate of $8 hourly. Driving to businesses to get them to purchase our products."

As soon as the words came out of his mouth, I am positive that my jaw dropped just slightly. He would want to cut my pay in half, and not only that but not pay me for mileage or commission. I could not take the position based on the money alone, and I am positive that he knew that going in.

From then on, the meeting progressed to severance and my last week. He stated that he would speak to the former investor about a severance package, and that we would meet later in the week to discuss it. Of course I knew as soon as the words left his lips that we would be meeting on my last day to discuss it, but from his initial thoughts it would be either two or three weeks of dismissal pay, no benefits, no options. I also took the opportunity in the meeting to question what my schedule would be since there was not much to do, and he told me to work the full day on Monday and that we would play it by ear. I told him that I would work the full day

Monday, but would take half days the remainder of the week and he agreed.

Driving away from that meeting, I can honestly say that I don't think I was as happy as I was in that moment since one of my more lucrative Christmas mornings as a child. I called my parents, called my roommate, called anyone that would listen, and for the first time in months, actually looked forward to going to work.... not that there was much work to actually be done anymore. The way I saw it, I had about three days' worth of completion work to do, and it would be smooth sailing from there.

My final full day was Monday, September 16th. I tied up all of my loose ends within the first few hours, and was then left wondering what could be done for the remainder of the week. This left me doing nothing more than filing and cleaning, as that was really all I *could* do to utilize my time and not waste entire days on the internet. I was still getting paid, after all.

I barely spoke to Randy or Shane throughout the duration of my final three days on the job. I came in, did what I had to, and left. Finally, on Wednesday the 18th, Randy came upstairs.

"You know this is the last day, right?"

We had not discussed it, but I was not about to look a gift horse in the mouth.

At that point, we went over what I had been spending my time doing and where things were, as well as the completion of my severance check. The final check was for my last two weeks of work, as well as the two weeks of severance pay that had been discussed in our meeting over the weekend. I requested the severance package in writing, but Randy denied, stating that he couldn't sign anything regarding my severance. As uneasy as this made me, I didn't care as long as I got the money I'd been promised.

At the conclusion of my last day on the job, I handed my keys to Randy and was barely given a goodbye, much less a good luck or thank you for the time I spent employed by the company. He would not even look at me. It wasn't what I was expecting, but at the same time, it was. They didn't like me, I didn't like them. I headed down the elevator with a smile on my face. As soon as I got downstairs to my apartment, I shot gunned a beer to celebrate. I was finally out of the worst job I ever had.

AFTERMATH

It took little more than a day before I received a text message from Randy asking where I'd placed a check that we had received from a customer. I answered, telling him that I had put it in his mailbox before leaving. He still stated that he couldn't find it. He went so far as to asking me if it was folded or flat. Both confused and utterly flabbergasted, I handed my phone to my roommate who texted back, "Flat. Flat like a check." That was the end of that one.

On September 20th, I received yet another message from Randy, telling me that the former investor needed to approve my severance check before it could be given to me and that I could go pick it up, but could not have it until it was okayed. Knowing what I'd been dealing with for over the past year, I knew that this could not be taken at face value. I thought through every possible scenario in 'the game', before the most obvious popped up: they wanted to see the check so that they could get the check number, put a stop payment on it, and not pay me severance at all. While it would be a firestorm for them, they did not care. Instead of replying, I went with my gut and picked the check up that morning, immediately bringing it to the bank where it was drawn and cashing it before bringing the appropriate paperwork back to Randy's apartment and leaving it outside his door. It was short and sweet, that and I didn't have to see Randy ever again – unless, of course, I had a stroke of bad luck and saw him in the elevator. After dropping the paperwork off at Randy's door, I went to take care of some bills and received yet another text from my former boss:

"Liz. That was a bad thing to do. Very bad."

How could cashing my own severance check be a bad thing? It had been discussed and written to me, and all parties had agreed to both the amount and circumstances before I picked it up. Boggled, I didn't bother to reply to the text message, but instead almost had both Randy and Shane's numbers blocked from my cell phone, as I was envisioning a barrage of texts and phone calls. After that, I did not receive another. I breathed easy for the first time in about a year and a half.

In the state of Wisconsin, an employee can file for unemployment based on a number of criterion, and being offered a position incomparable to a current position is one of them. Following the two weeks my dismissal pay covered, I chose to file for unemployment benefits as I was finding no luck in gaining other employment. Not that I thought it would be easy given the condition of the economy, but I had made a valiant attempt. I had never applied for unemployment before, and never really been unemployed for more than a month in my entire adult life, so had never needed to. I received all of the necessary paperwork from the state prior to my first week of paid benefits, and understood that I would receive benefits unless my claim was appealed. Which it was.

I expected it, knowing that they were angry with me for cashing my severance check. After filing my claim for the second week, I was alerted to the fact that they appealed my initial claim, and that it would need to be investigated by a state benefits adjudicator. The only difficult part was waiting the two weeks for the adjudicator's phone call, watching the food in my refrigerator dwindle further and further as the days passed. I finally received the phone call on a Monday morning.

The adjudicator stated that he had spoken to Shane, and that Shane had informed him that I had been offered a position at eleven dollars hourly for fifty-hour weeks. This was not what had been offered to me, and I stated that to the adjudicator, also stating that I had asked for the terms of the new position as well as my severance in writing and had been denied. He stated that he did not need to see the paperwork I had, and said that I would find out his decision soon.

One thing that I was interested in in this situation was the fact that Shane had not been in the meeting where my severance and the new position were discussed, and Shane was not my direct supervisor. Far be it for Randy to do anything for himself, I figured.

On the Wednesday of the same week, I received an automatic payment to my bank account for the two back weeks of claims. Without the form in hand, I knew that I'd won the appeal, and that finally – nearly a month later – I was finally done with 'the game', and finally done with Randy and Shane.

www.ingramcontent.com/pod-product-compliance
Lightning Source LLC
Chambersburg PA
CBHW031425210526
45464CB00005B/2057